300,000 Kisses

TALES OF QUEER LOVE FROM THE ANCIENT WORLD

Seán Hewitt &
Luke Edward Hall

PARTICULAR BOOKS
an imprint of
PENGUIN BOOKS

I

Eros, too, wakes with the season, as Earth
rolls through spring, and ignites with flowers.
Then the god departs from Cyprus, and goes
among men, scattering seed on the ground.

II

Boy, you're like a horse: already sated
with seed, you've come back to my stable now
longing for a good rider, an open meadow,
a crystal stream, a shaded grove.

THEOGNIS, *ELEGIES*

PROLOGUE

SEÁN HEWITT

In the two brief lyrics by the Ancient Greek poet Theognis which open this book, we get a first glimpse into the sunlit classical Mediterranean. In one poem, the springtime, and the blooming of the flowers, becomes the blossoming of love and desire. It moves across the land, mysterious and sacred. In the other poem, a boy is like a horse, full of muscular heat, drawn with urgency back to his lover. These verses are frank and tender. They give us sight of a world long before our own, where queerness was not only acknowledged, but shown to be utterly part of the fabric of life. The erotic takes place alongside the elemental; nature governs the passions; everything is full of longing and it is only right that we are too.

It is natural, when we don't see ourselves reflected in the world around us, to look for another world. It is natural, when we feel alone, to seek connection. All of us look for a past, but what happens when, gazing back in time, we see a world without us? That idea of a world without us is a lie, and the gaps in its history are no accident. But history is not the past, only the way it is written. Look closer, look longer, and what might first appear as a black sky suddenly seems to sparkle with a hundred constellations.

For queer people, the act of recovering history has often been one of discovering it, too. Is it any wonder that, placed on the dock during his trial for gross indecency, Oscar Wilde spoke of a love common to Plato, and Michelangelo, and Shakespeare? History and culture were proof of an enduring love that could produce some of the greatest works of art his audience knew. Picking up that golden thread, and placing himself as one of its inheritors, was an audacious and supremely affecting move. Many people in the court gallery, almost in spite of themselves, applauded.

Those names Wilde spoke of may be familiar to you, but I invite you to add the names of the characters and writers in this book, too. It is a long and glorious list. Every queer person has this same past, and deserves to inherit it. That sudden outbreak of applause in the courtroom is a glimpse of what it is like to witness a birthright brilliantly reclaimed. It takes our breath away, and its power resonates far and wide. It is that same radical and revelatory feeling I experience when I read these queer tales from the ancient world. I find that, rather than being cast out on the dark tide of history, I am sailing in a ship of gold.

When I first read that speech by Oscar Wilde as a teenager, I felt like the world, and my place within it, was forever changed. I found a hoard of jewels hidden from public view: a vibrant, justifying life beckoning me with what felt like a promise of belonging. When I heard whisperings about Ancient Greek culture at school, I felt like I was being told a secret. Those scraps of history felt illicit, mysterious, thrilling. I went off in pursuit of as much evidence as I could get my hands on, finding queer heroes and heroines and reading myself through them as I went. I came across Achilles first, a warrior whose name I knew because a part of my own body was named after him. Even a tendon in my own heel linked me into a queer story that no one had ever mentioned to me before. My heel was just like his, my body an heir to myth.

Through other traces, I picked up on this secret history. That golden thread is stitched throughout our culture's ideas of queerness: think, for example, of the very terms 'Sapphic', 'Lesbian' and 'androgynous', all of which have classical roots and inferences. As you read these tales, you will find many ways in which queer love and desire are woven all the way through the ancient world. They are carved into stones, and take their places among the flowers and the animals; they are an equal and fundamental part of those epics which have shaped the history and imagination of entire cultures.

There are some very contemporary questions provoked by reading these classics. Who do we imagine love for? Who do we credit with desire? On whom do we bestow the gift of immortality? Can the body be changed to better suit the soul inside? By picking up these questions in our own time, and by tracing them back through the tales of the ancients, we see new pathways, new pasts, and new ways of moving forward. What we find is the illumination of a world that completely overthrows the puritanism of our own. The exuberant frankness of the Greeks and Romans makes a mockery of how narrow our popular vision is, even now.

But things are, as always, not so simple. Though the writings in this book showcase much discussion of beauty, camaraderie and desire, there is also material not so easily assimilated into modern progressive thinking. A variety of gender roles and gender identities emerge in both the Roman and the Greek worlds, but they are not universally celebrated. Reading these new versions of the classics, you might find yourself seeking to map our own language and understandings on to this past. It is hard to move the words we use for our identities back in time – each arises out of its own historical context. Still, while the ancients might not have had concepts like ours (gay, or bisexual, or queer, or trans), the essential humanity tempts us to draw links, and of course there are careful links to be drawn. There are divine transformations of boys into girls and vice versa, there is an attention given to the 'androgyne' or 'hermaphrodite', and a focus on the ways some sexual desires and identities are accepted, and others curtailed by the societies of the ancients.

Of course, any representation of sex and desire has to make room for fantasy, and for the power dynamics of the gaze, and it is difficult to know what women, gender non-conforming people and persons of the lower classes would have made of these tales. In Martial's *Epigrams*, for instance, we meet two impressive butch women, Philaenis and Bassa. The gaze of the writer is both enthralled by their power and also keen to censure their rejection of men. He is both aroused and irritated. As modern readers, we catch a peek into this queer world, all the while being made aware of the misogyny that frames it. We also recognize a similar tendency in the modern male gaze: the objectification of women coupled with a terror of their sexuality.

The relationships between queer women are much less well documented in the literature of the Greek and Latin classics. Even in this book, where we bring you new versions of texts about what we might now call gender non-conforming characters and queer women, the insights are often fragmentary. Sappho's pulsing fragments are hymns to women beloveds, and a rare graffiti poem from Pompeii attests to the ways in which female desire and relationships were passed through song and stone. A love spell found on papyrus from Egypt shows the incantatory depths of female desire, full of energy and passion; and the tale of Iphis and Ianthe, from Ovid's *Metamorphoses*, plays with gender roles and the love between women.

The complex perspectives and receptions of these texts (these are tales told through the lens of satire, debate, and across a gulf of both real and imagined time) leave room to debate what is being endorsed, and what is being sanctioned. The ancient world is not a perfect mirror, nor is it one that offers uncomplicated images. Class, gender and sexual proclivity were then, as they still are, recognized as barriers to full freedom and acceptance. It is important to be aware of the imperfections and the alterity of these idealized societies, as well as to revel in their passionate music.

In these pages, you will likely find yourself moved, celebrated and troubled in equal measure. There are moments of tantalizing closeness between the reader and these passages, and moments of shocking distance. Importantly, we have not censored these texts. Though many have a history of being erased from modern editions (as with some of Martial's 'obscene' epigrams on homoerotic desire between women), we present them here in all their messy glory.

It struck me, as I was reading these texts, how often the stories, which regularly end in tragedy, subsume the beloved into the world of the gods, or hold the shape of their bodies in flowers that return each year, or in constellations that outlast any mortal. Their queerness, and their endurance, is wrapped up in myth-making, in origin stories, so that the world around us might be seen as the product of desire, yearning, and the deep grief of separated lovers. The characters are moved by the gods, by their passions, and by nature's changing seasons. Women turn into flowers, and etch their longing into stone; men inscribe their tears into petals, frequent steamy bathhouses and carve dildos from the branches of trees growing from the tombs of their old lovers. The gods, painfully in love with mortals, grieve and turn them into constellations. In this way, queer love is written through the landscape and through the heavens, deeply connected to the world it exists in, running a bright thread of longing across the intervening years. When we consider the many and ongoing erasures of queer history, the baffling silences of the archives, it is deeply moving to see a world, far off from our own, with queerness flowing through its very fabric.

It is our hope that, in this anthology, you might find romance, joy, tragedy, grief, desire, and connect again with these archetypal myths of queerness. This is no utopia, but it does acknowledge, unashamedly, the rich variousness of the human and the divine. In these sun-bleached shores and deep, lush groves, there is space for celebration and for the ecstatic dancing of the passions. If a hyacinth might be an inscription of queer love, or the stars in the sky an immortalization of queer desire, perhaps the way you see the world might be changed by these tales of heroes, heroines, sex workers, gods and demigods. Theirs is a vivid chorus, prophetic and time-bound, bleak and colourful. In this book, for the first time, we have tried to capture some of the dazzling queer energy of the ancients in image and in story, and to bring it, like a treasure, across the vast millennia, and into your hands.

GANYMEDE
& ZEUS

OVID, *METAMORPHOSES*

Ganymede was described by Homer as the most beautiful mortal man. He was abducted and brought to Olympus so that the gods could enjoy his radiant good looks. The myth of Ganymede and Zeus – of a young shepherd brought away by the most powerful god – served as an archetype for the Greek custom of pederasty (the romantic relationship between an adult male and an adolescent male), and there are countless depictions of Zeus, in the form of an eagle, abducting the youth. In some, the beautiful shepherd's dogs bark at the shadows of the clouds, trying to call him back to earth. In Rembrandt's painting of the scene, the youth is depicted as a toddler who urinates in fear as the monstrous eagle grips his arm. In Michelangelo's *Ganymede*, the muscular youth is pinioned by the eagle, who straddles him in a whirl of strength and violence, hurrying him up, struggling, into the sky. Ovid's brief account has little of this violence, and attends to the outline of the story itself. Here, in Ovid's Latin, the god Jupiter, often regarded as the Roman equivalent of Zeus, is referenced in Zeus' place.

The king of the gods once burned with love
for a youth named Ganymede. Jupiter searched
the world for a form to take, and lighted on a bird –
but no sparrow, no, only an eagle would do.
Only an eagle could carry the god's electric bolts
of lightning, and so he flew, on lying wings,
and swooped down on the clefted air and stole
the handsome boy, who now, despite the anger
of Juno, mixes the god's nectar and pours it
into Jupiter's cup.

A SHEPHERD'S SONG

VIRGIL, *ECLOGUES*

In this lush, love-filled pastoral, Virgil introduces us to a shepherd, Corydon, who is going mad with desire for a handsome young man named Alexis. The *Eclogues*, of which there are ten, are modelled on Greek bucolic poetry, but in Virgil's poems there is a turbulence afoot, whether political or, as in this case, erotic. They are full of singing shepherds. In fact, these poems were performed to popular acclaim on the Roman stage, and you can feel their dramatic quality here: the way the reader imagines Alexis without ever meeting him, the way Corydon, the singer, introduces us to the brimming summer landscape and to the history of his romantic life. Unlike the teeming, sunlit world around him, overgrowing with greenery and with fruit, Corydon is alone, without a lover, and the contrast between his longing and the silent figure of Alexis gives the poem a striking poignancy, built as it is around an absence.

O Corydon was on fire for Alexis –
his limbs, his heart burned on fantasy,
a hopeless cinder cooled only by the solace
of the thick beech groves, their soothing
shade on the hillsides where he walked
each day, and flung his tired songs,
poor shepherd, longing to be heard:

'Alexis, can you hear me?
One day the furnace of my mind will burn out
if you do not answer me. I'll die of love, I'm sure.
It's late afternoon, and the cattle are courting the shade

of the trees and the lizards are cooling
in the refuge of the brakes. The reapers, sunburnt
and tired, are being soothed with wild garlic
and with thyme – but you are gone. Hours I've spent
trailing your footsteps through the copse,
but the hot day rings only with the voice
of the cicadas, and with mine. God, listen to me.
Maybe I should have settled for another lover.
Maybe I should have borne Amaryllis' sulks,
her snarkiness, or made do with Menalcas,
though his looks were nothing to yours. Still,
Alexis, remember how the white blossom
of the privet falls; how the dark hyacinths
break under their own bloom …

'You look down on me, Alexis,
but I have a thousand lambs roaming the Sicilian hills
and not a summer or a winter goes by
when I am short of anything but you. I can sing
as Amphion used to sing, calling his cattle home
from the slopes of Aracynthus. And I think
I am fair, too; or at least my reflection was
a few days back when, with the wind stilling
the waves, I looked at myself in the hushed
mirror of the sea and liked what I saw. Imagine
if we could live here, together, Alexis –
in a cottage somewhere in the rough fields,
the two of us hunting deer, steering the flocks
into the green meadows of mallow-flower.

'Here, like Pan, you'd fill the woods
with song. Ah, to think of the music your full lips
could make! I have an instrument made

of hemlock stalks Damoetus on his deathbed
gave to me. "You will be its second lover," he said.
Amyntas was jealous of me then. I have two roe deer
I'm keeping for you, Alexis: I found them
in a harsh valley, stippled with white flanks.
They're still young, still feeding on ewes' milk,
and they could be yours, Alexis, if you came to me.

'O love, come here. Look! The nymphs
are bringing flowers for you, they are bringing baskets
of lilies. For you, the Naiad has picked a spray
of iris and poppy-heads, of yellow narcissus
and sweet fennel-flower. Look how she twines them
with cassia and with herbs, with bilberries
and marigold. And I would gather quinces for you,
their pale and velvet fruit, and chestnuts too,
like I did for Amaryllis when I loved her. And you,
ripe plums, and you, laurel branches, and you,
sweet myrtle. O Corydon, you fool! If Alexis
cared at all, it would not be for gifts.
Iollas could beat you at gift-giving anyway.
You are a fool to have such dreams, and now
in your stupid singing you've let the wind unpick
your flowers, you've let the wild boar trample
your crystal spring.

'Who are you running from? Even Paris
lived in the woods like me. Let Pallas live alone
in her empty citadels. I love the woodlands
more than any other place. It goes like this, Alexis:
the lioness pursues the wolf, the wolf pursues
the goat, the goat goes after the flowering clover,
and I go after you. Look – the hanging ploughs

are feathering the fields, and the sinking sun
doubles the length of the bullock's shadow –
but still, still, after all my singing, love tears a fire
through me. It scorches me. It has no limit
and no relief. Ah, Corydon, still this lunacy,
this possession. Look at you. Half your vines
are unclipped, half the elms are overrun.
Why not settle? Why not get some work done?
Surely, sad shepherd, if Alexis won't come,
surely you'll find another?'

LAMENT
GRAFFITI

CORPUS INSCRIPTIONUM LATINARUM

This graffiti – one of the few poems with a woman speaker addressing a woman lover to survive from the ancient Roman world – was found on a wall in a hallway in Pompeii. The plaster on which it was written, in neat lines of metrical text, is now held in the National Archaeological Museum of Naples. It is likely that the poem was inscribed here not by the original author, but by someone who had heard the poem, remembered it, and wanted to write it down.

The final image of the lament makes it almost an aubade – a poem which greets the rising of the sun and laments the passing of the night, when lovers in bed must wake, separate, and go their own ways into the world. Many readers might associate this type of poem with the love lyrics of the Renaissance, but its particular moment – poised between light and dark, between private intimacy and public life – is delicately rendered here, too.

O, if only I could hold your arms around my neck
and press a thousand kisses to your tender lips –
but go, little doll, throw your happiness to the breeze …
Trust me, men are fickle things.
Often, I find myself awake in the middle of the night,
lost somehow in thought, seeing all the people fortune
has lifted up. She throws them down eventually,
her little dolls. See, even now, Venus has joined
the bodies of lovers, but then the daylight comes
and prises them apart …

THE TALE OF
A THREESOME

LUCIAN, *DIALOGUE OF THE COURTESANS*

In this dialogue, set among a cast of sex workers, a woman recounts the tale of a threesome with Megilla and her wife, Demonassa. We might think of Megilla as a butch, or as 'a woman with the mind and desires of a man', as she tells Leaina, but Megilla's descriptions of herself do not fall within the language available to the courtesans. Elsewhere, she rejects the idea of being a woman at all, suggesting other possible identities, and recent scholarship has suggested we might better refer to Megilla with male pronouns, as a trans man. That certainly seems to fit the bill, and I have maintained she/her pronouns here merely to carry the complexity of the original into English. Though Leaina tries to fit Megilla into a definition, Megilla shirks it, correcting her openly. It gives us an insight into the Romans' conception of gender and sexuality, and we feel it bristling at the binary.

Though Lucian's audiences had a rigid view of gender as biologically determined, and would have read Megilla as a woman, perhaps Lucian's characterization reveals the limitations of that narrow view. Something else we notice here is the frankness and lack of shame with which sex work is treated, though there is coyness regarding queer desire. In the frame of this story, Clonarion presses Leaina for more information, which she yields before becoming embarrassed by her same-sex experiences. It's a playful, sexy and free-spirited scene.

CLONARION: I've been hearing strange rumours about you, Leaina. People are saying that Megilla, the rich woman from Lesbos, loves you as though she were a man and that she ... well, that you and her do god knows what together. What? Are you blushing? So it's true ...

LEAINA: It's the truth, Clonarion. But I'm so ashamed. It's against nature.

CLONARION: In the name of Aphrodite, Leaina! Tell me everything. What does the woman ask of you? What do the two of you do together? Tell me!

LEAINA [blushing, looks down at her feet in silence]

CLONARION: Well, now I'm sure you don't love me. If you did, you wouldn't keep secrets from me.

LEAINA: Clonarion, don't say that. I love you as much as I love any woman. The thing is, Megilla is quite like a man.

CLONARION: I'm not sure I understand … Unless you mean she's a sort of … ladies' woman? I've heard there are women like that in Lesbos. Women with faces like men but who won't suffer the beds of men, women who find pleasure with other women, as though they themselves were men. Is that what Megilla is like?

LEAINA: Something like that, yes.

CLONARION: Well, come on! Less of these short replies. I want to hear it all, Leaina. How did she come on to you? How did she persuade you to let her have her way with you? And what happened after that?

LEAINA: Well, it happened when Megilla and another woman, Demonassa of Corinth, were organizing a drinking party, and they brought me with them, so that I might provide music to set the scene. But, as soon as I had finished my last song, when the night was late and the women were drunk and I was tired, Megilla turned to me and said, 'Come along, Leaina, you look tired. Why not sleep here between the two of us?'

CLONARION: And did you? And then what happened?

LEAINA: First, they pulled me close and kissed me like men do, not just with their lips, but with their mouths apart, their breath in mine, holding me and my breasts. Demonassa even bit me gently as she kissed, and I hardly knew what to make of it. After a while, Megilla, her skin hot against mine, flushed and sweating, pulled off her wig. I was amazed: I had never suspected her hair was false, but underneath she revealed her close-shaven head, just as an athlete's head might be.

She must have seen my shock, and said, 'Leaina, have you ever seen such a handsome fellow?' 'I don't see a fellow here, Megilla,' I answered. 'Don't make a woman of me,' she said. 'I've been married to Demonassa here for a long time. She is my wife.' I laughed at that, Clonarion, and said, 'Then, Megilla, I hadn't known you were a man all this time. Is it like when Achilles hid himself among the girls? Or do you have everything a man has? Do you play the part of a man with Demonassa?' 'I haven't got what you mean,' she replied. 'I don't need a cock. As you'll find out, I have a much more pleasant method of my own.'

'Surely you're not a hermaphrodite, with both a man's and a woman's tools, as many people are said to have?' I swear, Clonarion, I still didn't know what was happening. But she said, 'No, Leaina, I'm all man.'

'Well,' I replied, 'I was once told by Ismenadora, a Boeotian flute player who often repeated tales to me, that

someone from Thebes had once been changed from a woman into a man. A good truth-teller named Tiresias. Did something like that happen to you, too?'

'No, Leaina. I was born a woman just the same as the rest of you, but I have the mind and the desires of a man.'

'And do you find that those desires are enough for you?' I asked.

'If you don't believe me,' Megilla replied, 'I can prove it to you. Just give me the chance, and you'll soon find out I'm as good as any man. I have a toy that resembles a man's equipment. Just give me half a chance, and I'll show you.'

And, well, I gave her the chance, if only because she pleaded so much and gave me presents: a fine necklace, and a dress of the cleanest linen. And so I threw my arms around her as though she were a man, and she kissed me deeply, panting as she worked, and giving moans of pleasure herself.

CLONARION: And what did she do? How did it work? I want to hear it all, Leaina!

LEAINA: Now, don't press me any further for the details. I'm ashamed of them! By the name of Aphrodite, I won't say one more word about it.

ARISTOPHANES ON LOVE

PLATO, *THE SYMPOSIUM*

Plato's *Symposium* (*c.* 385–370 BC) gives us one of the most enduring myths we have about the origins of love. The book itself depicts a number of speeches, each given by a notable man attending a banquet. Amongst these men, who include Socrates, the legal expert Pausanias and Eryximachus the physician, is the comic playwright Aristophanes. The latter succumbs to a fit of hiccups during the rest of the speeches, but finally is able to add his own voice to the conversation, putting forward a creation myth, seeking to explain the sense of wholeness we find when we meet our beloveds, or 'our other half'. Moving from the bizarre and the grotesque through to a theory of worship and unity, it is a brilliant and unforgettable achievement.

First of all, you must learn about human nature and its history. For, in ancient times, our nature was not as it is now, but of another kind. To begin with, there were not just two sexes, as we have now, but three. Aside from male and female, there was a third sex, which had aspects of both male and female in common. This third sex was androgynous, both in form and in nature, and now only the name of it is remembered, and often it is used as an insult.

And there is another thing I must tell you. The form of each human was round, with the back and the sides forming a circle. The human had four arms and four legs, and had two faces, both identical, on either side of a cylindrical neck. Each face was turned in the opposite direction from the other. The human had four ears, and two sets of genitals, and I'm sure you can imagine the rest. They walked upright, as we do now. When they ran, they were swift, moving on all eight limbs, and they somersaulted, too, tumbling and rolling in cartwheels.

There was a reason for having these three sexes. The sun was the original parent of the male, and the earth was the original parent of the female, and the moon was the parent of the third sex, being a combination of the sun and the earth together. These humans were round and moved in this circling fashion because they took after their parents. The offspring of the sun, earth and moon were formidable in their strength and force and, because of the ambition of their thoughts, they began to conspire against the gods. Homer told us this, and Ephialtes and Octus told us too: the humans tried to storm the gates of Heaven; they tried to displace the gods.

Zeus and the other Olympians gathered to discuss a plan of action. None of them could decide what path was best. They couldn't kill the humans, like they did the Giants, whose race they wiped out with thunderbolts. After all, the humans made offerings and sacrifices to the gods, and if they killed the humans, those honours would disappear too. Still, they couldn't sit by and watch as the humans acted so egregiously.

Then, after much hard thinking, an idea came to Zeus. 'I think I have a plan,' he said. 'There is a way to make the humans weaker. They could continue to exist, but they would be too diminished to carry on with their boldness. My plan is to cut each of them in half. Think about it. This way, they'll be weaker, and they'll also be more useful to us, since there will be twice as many of them. They could still walk upright on their two legs, so that won't be a problem. And if they still carry on misbehaving, I'll cut them in half again, and watch them hop around on the one leg they have left.'

The gods thought it was worth a try, so Zeus went straight to work. He cut the humans in two, just as you might cut a sorb apple in half, or slice an egg through the middle with a wire. After that, he told Apollo to turn the face and the split neck of each human towards the place where the wound was made, so that each person should see the place of his division and be chastised. Apollo healed the remaining wounds: he drew together all the skin over the long wound of each person, over what we now call the torso, just as a purse is closed by a drawstring and, tying it in the centre, made a single puckered opening, which now we call the navel. He worked over the rest of the skin with a tool, like the tool used by shoemakers to smooth leather, but he left the wrinkles on the navel to serve as a reminder of this ancient suffering.

Now that their natures were divided in two, each human half would rush in longing to its other half. The gods saw them throwing their arms around each other, intertwining them, longing to grow into one another, to form a single living thing. The new humans began to die of hunger, of depression, because none of them wanted to live without the other, or to do anything on their own. Whenever one half of the original whole died, the one that was left went in search of another and wove itself together with that. Sometimes the one it met was half of a whole female (the half we now call 'a woman'), and other times it was half of a male. Either way, the people continued to perish.

Zeus, watching them, was moved to pity. It was time for a change in the plan, and he came up with a modified version of the human, moving their genitals around to the front of

their bodies. Before that, the people had to breed on the soil, laying their children in the damp earth, as locusts do – but now, in the new form, they could use the warmth of their own bodies. If a male half met a female half, their embrace would give rise to children. And if a male met another male, there would at least be the pleasure of being inside one another, and each would be relieved, and be able to go back to work, or to thinking about life. It was in this way that love for each other was sown into human beings. They were given a birthright of desire, and a way of fulfilling it in the body of another. Eros, you see, would bring their ancient natures together, making one whole from two halves. In this way, the old division would be healed.

Each of us, then, is just half of a human – we have been sliced in two like flatfish, and each of us seeks our matching half. Those men who are cleaved from the common sex, the androgynous, desire women; often, these men are adulterous. Similarly, women who are attracted to men and are adulteresses come from this sex. Those sectioned from an original male pursue other men, because they themselves are male, and from a young age they desire to lie with men, and to be embraced by them. These are by nature the most masculine and the most noble people. Some say that they have no shame, but they are wrong: they do not seek other men out of shamelessness, but out of boldness, courage and

masculine virtue. They unite with what is like themselves, and with those who share their qualities. Here is some proof: when these men grow up, they often enter into political life. From manhood, they love boys, and by their nature pay no attention to marriage or to the custom of having children, except when compelled to it. They are happy to live out their lives unmarried, and to spend their time in each other's company. So, this kind is wholly a lover of boys, and is always seeking what is akin to themselves.

When a lover of boys, or any other type of person, meets the one who is their other half, each is overwhelmed with friendship and kinship and desire, and they can hardly bear to be separated for even a small amount of time. These are the people who will spend whole lifetimes together. They can hardly say what they wish for themselves when the other is absent. No one could be so mistaken as to think that it is for sex alone that these couples love each other: the soul of each of them, like a holy oracle, sings and desires something beyond words.

Imagine that Hephaestus with his tools stood over them as they lay together and asked, 'What is it that you want from each other?' And suppose they were perplexed by the question, and Hephaestus continued: 'Is it your desire to be in the same place as each other, and never parted in either the night or the day? If it is, I could fuse you together, welding you so that both of you become one, and you might share a common life as long as you live, and when you die you will arrive into the Place of the Dead as one, and share even death in common. Is this what you long for?'

We know that no lover who heard this would refuse it, no lover would wish for anything else. Any lover, hearing these words, would think that they had heard spoken the very thing they had always desired. The reason is as I have said: that in our ancient nature, we were whole. Eros, then, is another name for the pursuit of wholeness. Just as we were once whole, we have now been dispersed by the gods because of our crimes, just as the Arcadians have been by the Spartans. So the fear remains that, if we choose a life of chaos over harmony, we will be divided again by the gods. We will go around the world like the figures carved in tombstones, sawn in half down the nose. We will be born like split dice.

This is why all of us should urge each other to worship the gods, so that we may escape that fate and follow, instead, Love as our guide and our leader. No one should go contrary to Love. Anyone who does is despised by the gods. Only by becoming friends of the gods, by reconciling ourselves with them, will we discover our own beloveds.

Hush, Eryximachus. Don't interrupt me, or laugh at what I am saying. It isn't only aimed at Pausanias and Agathon. True, those two men may be of the kind I am talking about, and are both masculine by nature – but what I am saying applies to everyone, the whole human race. This is how we will become happy, by allowing Love to reach its journey's end, so that each of us might find our beloved and restore our original nature.

If this is for the best, then it follows that it suits us best to encourage everyone to meet their beloved, the one who is most like to them in mind and in character. We should sing the praises of Eros, who in the present day brings us into the knowledge and company of what is properly our own. Eros, or Love, is the one who brings us our greatest hope, and promises to return us to our original state, to heal us, to bless us, and to bring us perfect happiness.

HYACINTHUS & APOLLO

OVID, *METAMORPHOSES*

Ovid's *Metamorphoses* is one of the most influential poems in Western culture. Over the course of fifteen books, Ovid relates more than two hundred and fifty myths. Its principal theme, as the poet tells us in his opening line, is how bodies are changed, moved from one form to another. Often, in times of distress or threat, the human characters in the book are transformed into other elements of nature: trees, birds, springs and constellations.

Hyacinthus, the hero and lover of Apollo, god of the sun, is another of the beautiful mortals of Greek mythology. Apollo is so transfixed by Hyacinthus that he gives up his shrine at Delphi to descend to earth and be with him, teaching the man how to play the lyre and how to shoot an arrow. As Ovid points out in the opening of this passage, Hyacinthus might have had a similar fate to Ganymede, had it not been for a brutal misfortune. In some accounts, Zephyrus (the west wind) is also in love with Hyacinthus, and is so jealous of Apollo that he blows the god's discus off course in order to kill the young man. In Ovid's version, the death of Hyacinthus is figured as an accident, a tragic mischance, and is made all the more resonant for that. Such slips of fate might rob any lovers of their happiness, their promised life together, and the scene that follows is full of moving desperation, with even Apollo, the god, seeking solace in the image of flowers as a form of rebirth and of eternal life.

You too, Hyacinthus, might have been lifted
into the sky, had it not been for the fates –
but you, too, are immortal, in a way. When winter
leaves off, and spring comes, and Aries
takes the place of the Pisces, you bloom again

in the fresh grass. The love my father, Apollo,
had for you, was deeper than for anyone else.
He forsook his shrine at Delphi, the earth's navel,
and took to haunting the city of Sparta, close
by the flowing river. He gave up his arrows
and his lyre, he forgot all the things that once
had brought him joy, and instead he carried
Hyacinthus' nets, and held the leash of his hounds,
and went with him, like a comrade, over the steep,
rough mountains. Every hour they spent together
fuelled his love, and once, when Titan was midway
between the banished and the coming night,
Apollo and Hyacinthus stripped, oiled themselves,
and challenged each other in the throwing
of a discus. First, Apollo: he positioned it well
then sent it flying through the air, cleaving
a white cloud with the heavy iron. So strong
and skilful was his throw that it was a long time
before the disc came back towards earth. Quickly,
without thinking, Hyacinthus rushed forward
to pick it up, but the plate wasn't done yet:
it landed curvewise on the hard soil, and rebounded
with force and struck into Hyacinthus' face.
Oh, Apollo went pale as the dead then, as pale
as his beautiful boy, who he caught in his arms
as he fell. With care, he lifted the huddled body,
held it close. Desperately he tried to warm the boy,
desperately he tried to staunch the blood,
to find a healing herb, but the wound
was past all cure. As when a broken violet
or a poppy in a garden hangs its heavy flower
and looks only at the earth, so the boy's face

drooped: his head bowed then fell
upon his shoulder. 'You are fading away,
Hyacinthus,' cried the god. 'I see your wound,
and I see my own guilt. Death has made you
my sorrow and my shame. It was my hand
that killed you, and the world will know it.
But all we did was play a game, all we did
was love each other. Can that be called a fault?
Hyacinthus, listen. Let me die in your place,
or die beside you. If this is death, let me
staunch it, let me hold it back: I will carry you
in my heart, recall you in my mouth, echo you
in song, play the notes of your name
on the lyre. As a new flower registers
the elements, I will score you into petals.'
And as Apollo spoke, the blood that spilled
from Hyacinthus darkened the grass
then resolved into a bloom, brighter
than Tyrian dye, and took the form
of a lily in purple. But that wasn't enough:
Apollo watched his miracle occur, and the cries
of grief that tore out of him were etched
into the flower, so it was patterned
with the letters of his lamentation.
The city of Sparta was never ashamed
of her son Hyacinthus, and even now his beauty
endures, returning each year to be greeted
by crowds and by a solemn festival.

WRITTEN
IN THE STARS

OVID, *FASTI*

Ovid's *Fasti*, an incomplete poem tracing the first six months of the Roman calendar, is sometimes translated as *The Book of Days*. Each book covers one month, beginning in January and moving through to June, and each is replete with myths and legends which illustrate the origins of Roman holidays and customs. Taken from the third book, this short poem relates the story of Ampelus, one of Bacchus' beloveds, who fell to his death while picking grapes. After Ampelus falls, Bacchus – here called Liber, the Romanized form of the Greek deity – immortalizes the boy in the stars, forming them into the shape of a grape-gatherer.

When, at the fifth dawn, Aurora
from her saffron cheeks begins the dropping
of the dew, the constellation will sink
out of sight. But it will not be so
for the Grape-Gatherer. There is a tale
behind that glittering star-shape. It is said
that Ampelus – the son of a nymph
and a satyr – was loved by Bacchus
who adored him on the Ismarian hills.
The god gave the boy a vine. It trailed
from the high boughs of an elm, and still
the vine takes its name from the youth.
One day, while he gathered the bright
ripening grapes from the branch, he lost
his grip, he called out and he fell – but Liber
caught him, and raised him up to the stars.

ACHILLES & PATROCLUS

HOMER, *THE ILIAD*

Achilles and Patroclus are two warriors central to the stories of the Trojan War. Achilles, who is often fierce and stony-hearted towards his fellow fighters, is gentle and loving towards Patroclus, and the two camp together. While later Christian writers suppressed the romantic and sexual aspects of their relationship, classical writers such as Aeschylus and Plato were explicit and heartfelt in holding the two men up as lovers.

After Patroclus was slain, Achilles led the Myrmidons in grieving for him. They drove their horses around his body, lamenting, until all the sand and their armour was wet with tears. The corpse of Hector was dragged around and defiled in anger and flung into the dust face-first beside Patroclus' funeral bier. Then Achilles began the feast, slaughtering so many oxen and goats that the blood pooled around the corpse, deep enough to dip a cup into.

Achilles, still grieving, was asked to dine with Agamemnon. 'In the name of Zeus,' he said, 'I will not wash the blood from my face and arms until I have lain Patroclus on the pyre, and shorn off my hair. I will allow time for food first, but at dawn we must gather wood, and set Patroclus on his journey to the afterlife.' After the meal, the company retired to rest, but Achilles lay around, sighing and mourning as the waves echoed and broke along the shore ...

Achilles' beautiful body was exhausted.
He had hunted Hector all the way to Illium –
where the gusts of wind had battered him –
and here, by the echoing sea, no sooner
had sleep wrapped him in its arms

than he saw a ghost. Was it Patroclus?
He looked the same, he spoke the same –
even the way he stood, the clothes he wore,
the look in his eyes, all of them seemed real,
like the real thing. 'You are asleep, Achilles,'
said the ghost, leaning gently over him.
'That must mean you have forgotten me.
You never forgot me when I was by your side.'
'Please,' the ghost said, weeping now. 'I cannot pass
the gates of Hades without a funeral. The phantoms
keep me out. They will not let me join them
beyond the river, and I'm left to wander alone
through cold rooms and corridors. Give me
your hand, Achilles, clasp hold of me.
Once my body is burned, I won't be able
to return to you. This is the last time
we can sit and talk apart from the others,
like we once did – just the two of us.
I have come to ask you something. When you die,
as you will beneath the walls of Troy,
let us be buried together, let us blend –
as we did when we were boys – into one.
Let one urn, the one your mother gave you,
hold us together, our bones and our dust.'
And Achilles looked up at him, full of grief
and confusion. 'Patroclus, my love,
I will do everything you ask. But come to me,
closer, come here to me. If only for a moment,
let us hold each other, let us comfort each other
one last time.' And Achilles reached out
to Patroclus, outstretching his hands
to the spirit, but as he closed his arms

they met around nothing – only air, only smoke –
and Patroclus was gone, and Achilles held
only himself. He wept bitterly then, hitting
his own body; and finally, exhausted
as the dawn lifted pink behind the waves,
he consoled himself, saying, 'At least now I know
that something survives in the halls of Hades –
some ghost, some resemblance of us lives on.
Tonight, comrades, Patroclus was here. I saw him.
I heard his voice, steering me. I felt, once more,
his beautiful shadow as it moved across me.'

So Achilles spoke, and his words stirred
all the men to tears, and rosy-fingered dawn
found them weeping around the dead.

THE SACRED BAND

PLUTARCH, *LIVES*, 'PELOPIDAS'

The Greek philosopher, historian and biographer Plutarch wrote an extensive series of biographies of famous men. They are called the *Lives*, and are made up of 'parallels', arranged in pairs, so that the life of one Roman and one Greek can be seen side-by-side, and compared for virtues and vices. Here, in his life of Pelopidas, an important Theban statesman, Plutarch tells us of a 'sacred band' – a regiment made up of one hundred and fifty pairs of lovers and their beloveds. The army formed the elite force of Thebes and won numerous battles, famous for its effectiveness and ferocity.

The afterlife of this passage in queer history is a rich and rousing one. Cut forward to 1990, and the New York branch of ACT UP, a grassroots protest group working through direct action and advocacy to end the AIDS pandemic, distributed a leaflet titled 'Queers Read This!' In bold lettering, it echoed the story of the 'sacred band'. It declared 'An Army of Lovers Cannot Lose: Everyone of us is a world of infinite possibility. We are an army because we have to be. We are an army because we are so powerful. (We have so much to fight for; we are the most precious of endangered species.) And we are an army of lovers because it is we who know what love is. Desire and lust, too. We invented them. We come out of the closet, face the rejection of society, face firing squads, just to love each other!'

It is said that the Sacred Band was founded by Gorgidas. Three hundred men were chosen – they were trained, and given their station on the Cadmea. This is why they were called the city regiment. According to some accounts, the troop was made up of lovers and their beloveds, of one hundred and fifty pairs of men. An old joke tells us that

Nestor paid too little attention to tactics when he told the Greeks to arrange their soldiers by clans and tribes. The wisdom went that clans should stand shoulder to shoulder, and the tribes likewise. But Nestor, the joke says, should have organized the army into groups of lovers instead.

See, when danger comes, tribes and clans can turn against each other, can leave the injured behind. But a band united by love – which cannot be broken or dissolved – cannot itself be broken or dissolved. When danger comes, an army of lovers stands its ground. The lover protects his beloved; the beloved protects his lover.

There is a story of a man who, lying on the ground, injured, with his enemy about to kill him, implored the enemy to drive a blade through his breast, so that his beloved would not have to see him die, and would not have to be ashamed of his injury. It was only natural, then, that the troop should have been called 'sacred', for Plato describes a lover as a friend who is 'inspired by the gods'.

The Sacred Band was never defeated until the battle of Chaeronea. When King Philip of Macedon was going through the bodies, after the fighting was ended, he walked over to the place where the three hundred lay dead in their armour, their bodies piled all on top of each other. And he stood there amongst them, amazed, and when he learned that the Band was an army of lovers, he wept, and called out a curse on anyone who might think that these men ever did anything shameful, or ever suffered anything shameful to be done to them.

SOCRATES ON LOVE

XENOPHON, *THE SYMPOSIUM*

Xenophon's *Symposium*, written around the year 360 BC, is a Socratic dialogue. This form of writing, which was an established and popular genre, consists of various characters – often real-life figures – debating points of philosophy. Through conversation, the underlying tenets of various ideas are pulled apart and analysed. In this passage from Xenophon's work, Socrates and a few of his friends are having a dinner party and discussing important subjects. Callias is the host, and the dinner is being thrown for Autolycus, whom Callias is in love with. After the entertainment departs, Socrates stands up to speak, and begins to talk about Love. There is clearly some drinking involved, and sometimes Socrates is heckled, and heckles back. In giving a general speech on Love and its qualities, however, it becomes clear that Socrates is in fact trying to help Callias in his pursuit of Autolycus, offering advice, and playing a sort of matchmaker.

After the Syracusian left, bathed in the sound of applause, Socrates once again embarked on a new subject.

'Gentlemen,' he said, 'we are in the presence of a great god – as eternal and ancient as any god, and yet this god is so fresh and youthful. Do you know who I am talking about? This god encompasses everything, infuses everything, and finds his home, his holy shrine, in the human heart. I am speaking, of course, of Love. Isn't it only right that we should be mindful of him and talk about him tonight, when all of us here are his followers? For my part, I cannot think of a time when I was not in love with someone, and I know that you, Charmides, have had many lovers, and have had your heart set aflame more than once. And you, Critobulus, haven't you been admired, and don't you still fall in love, even now? Niceratus, you too – I know you are in love with your wife, and that your love is wholly returned. As for you, Hermogenes, all of us can see that you are almost wasting away with love for an ideal, for a sense of beauty and virtue. Look at him: see how he knits his brow, how calm his eyes are, how temperate and measured he is in his speech, how gentle he is, how kind? Even though he loves the gods, and enjoys their blessings, he has not spurned his friends here on Earth. Is it only you among us, Antisthenes, who is not in love?'

'Not true!' Antisthenes replied. 'Aren't I in love with you, Socrates? Madly in love!'

Socrates giggled, ironically, pretending to be coy and girlish. 'Hush, don't pester me now. Can't you see I'm busy?'

'God, you're so transparent,' said Antisthenes. 'You're always dodging me, or making a joke. Half the time you use the gods as an excuse for not talking to me, and the other half it's because you fancy someone else.'

'For heaven's sake, Antisthenes, put your claws away. I can take it when you're sulking, or insulting me, but not this. Let's just draw a line under it. You only want me for my body, but I'm Socrates – I have a beautiful mind, too!

'Sorry for the interruption, everyone. Now, where was I? Ah yes, you, Callias. Everyone in the city knows you're in love with Autolycus. Actually, I think that news has gone overseas, too, thanks to your fathers both being famous, and you both being distinguished gents yourselves. I've always admired your character, Callias, but now I admire it even more. I can see that Autolycus is not a spoilt man, and is not ruined by effeminacy. Anyone who looks at him can see how strong, brave and disciplined he is, and that's a testament to your love, too, and shows that you are attracted to the right qualities in a man.

'Now, whether there is one Love or two, "Heavenly" or "Common", I do not know. Even Zeus has many names and titles, though he is the same god. But what I do know is that there are many different altars and many different shrines, and that the rites of those who follow Common Love are looser than the chaste rites of the Heavenly devotees. We might guess that those inspired by Common Love are more carnal, and those inspired by Heavenly Love are attracted to minds, and friendships, and nobility of character. That love, Heavenly Love, is the one that I think has inspired you, Callias – there is nothing base in Autolycus, and I've seen that, whenever you are together, you invite his father, too, knowing that there is nothing between you that is shameful or in need of concealment.'

'Socrates,' said Hermogenes, 'the thing I admire most about you – and there are many things to admire – is that, in the same breath as you compliment Callias, you also manage to instruct him in good morals.'

'That is what I hope to do,' Socrates replied. 'And I hope it will add to his pleasure in life, knowing that love for the mind is higher than physical love. After all, there is no conversation worth the name if it does not come from a place of affection.

'Now, it seems to me that those who are inspired by Heavenly Love, who admire the mind of their beloved, often experience their love as a pleasure; but those whose desires are only physical tend to criticize the characters of their beloveds. Even if they love both mind and body, the

passing of time is inescapable, and soon enough youth fades, and often the love of the body fades with it; but the mind only grows in wisdom over time, and so love of the mind grows with it. Besides, with physical love, after we are satisfied, we do not want it any more. But love for the soul, being pure, is also less likely to find completion. This does not mean that Aphrodite looks less warmly on it. On the contrary, she answers our prayers and makes us more charming because of them.

'Now, there is no need for me to argue that a soul verdant and in bloom, a soul fresh with reverence and authority, feels a rich affection for the object of its love; but what I will argue is that it is natural that such a soul should have its love reciprocated. For a start, who could possibly dislike a person who is the very pattern of goodness, and who he can see is more concerned about the honour of his beloved than about his own pleasure? And who could not be charmed by a love that is unalterable, unchanging even in the face of illness or the ageing body of the beloved? After all, lovers who love in deep affection must look into each other's faces lovingly; they must talk to each other lovingly; they must trust and be trusted; must share each other's sorrows and joys; and if either falls ill, the other must keep company, and care for him; and the two must care for each other even more when they are apart. This is the sort of love, the sort of devotion, that lasts a lifetime.

'But why should a boy return the affection of a lover who only admires him for his looks? Such a lover takes all the gratification, and leaves the boy all the shame. His love cuts the boy off from his family and friends, and what does the boy receive in return? The fact that such a lover uses persuasion makes him even worse. A lover who uses force proves that he is a villain, but a lover who uses persuasion and flattering words ruins the reputation of any boy who succumbs to him. A boy does not get any pleasure out of sex, as a woman might. When a man is making love to him, the boy is like a sober person watching a drunk. It should hardly surprise us if the boy comes to hate a lover like this. But if the lover was governed by Heavenly Love, and loved the boy's mind and character, only good things would follow.

'And now, moving on from the beloved, I must speak a little about the effects of this sort of love on the lover himself. Love of the body alone makes the lover servile. After all, the person who educates you should be held in honour, as Chiron and Phoenix were held in honour by Achilles; but the person who only wants your body, who follows you around, irritatingly, begging you for a kiss, or for a moment's embrace, is a sort of scrounger.

'Don't be surprised that I'm speaking so freely tonight. It's partly because I've had quite a few glasses of wine, and it loosens me up, but it's also because Love is my constant friend, and I feel the need to warn you about its adversary. It seems to me that a man who only desires his beloved's body is like a man who has rented a plot of land. He doesn't want to increase its value, but to extract value from it. His eyes are always on the harvest. But the man who desires the affection of his beloved is like a man who owns his own plot: he uses all his means, and everything in his power, to increase the worth of his beloved. Besides, a beloved who knows that he is only valued for his outward beauty will take little trouble over improving himself in other ways; but if he knows that, without improving in wisdom and virtue, he cannot keep his lover, he will work on these qualities. Likewise, the lover must work on his own virtue, so that he can lead by example.

'If we look at our myths, Callias, we can see that even the gods and demigods set the love of the mind above physical desire. Zeus loved many mortals, but it was only the ones that he loved for their minds that he made immortal after he was done with them. Heracles, for example, and the Dioscuri. I would argue that even the handsome Ganymede, famed for his beauty, was loved by Zeus for his mind, and it was this that led the god to carry him up to Olympus. And – are you listening, Niceratus? – Homer tells us that Achilles carried out his vengeance for Patroclus not just because Patroclus was beautiful, but because he was Achilles' friend, and the two held each other in deep affection. The same could be said of Orestes and Pylades, or Theseus and Pirithous, and many of the great heroes, who were inspired to their greatest acts not because they slept together, but because they loved each other.

'The same goes for the great acts of our own time. Is it not true that they are done for glory and the esteem of others, and are done by courageous people, rather than by those who put pleasure before valour? Think of Pausanias, and how he tells us about 'the sacred band', and how an army of lovers cannot lose. Not all of us agree with Pausanias' evidence – some of us no longer admire pederasty, and the Spartans think that all sexual desire corrupts a soldier – but either way, it is goodness that is valued above all things. Who would you rather trust with your money or your children, a beloved valued for his looks, or one loved for his mind?

'Callias, I have said all of this in order to say a simpler thing: that you should thank the gods for giving you your love for Autolycus. It is easy to see that he is an honourable man, and one with great courage and ambition. Now, if we imagine that it is not only his own and his father's honour that he desires, but also the ability to help his friends and to raise the honour of his country, wouldn't it be fair to say that he would be most likely to love a man who could help him achieve these things? So, if you want him to love you, and to hold you in affection, you should study, and find out what helped Themistocles to liberate Greece, and what sort of wisdom raised Pericles into his reputation as his country's wisest counsel, and how Solon made the finest laws for his city, and what the Spartans do to gain their renown as the best leaders in the world. Representatives of the Spartans come to your house, and it would be no surprise if your country placed you in the position of its leader. You are noble, you are the finest priest on festival days, and your body is the most beautiful of all the men in the city.

'I am sorry if you think I have spoken more earnestly tonight than is appropriate when there is wine to be drunk, but it can hardly surprise you. I have always been united with the commonwealth in loving good and virtuous men.'

After this speech, the other men as usual took the cue to discuss what Socrates had said, but Autolycus kept his eyes fastened for the whole time on Callias.

AN EMPEROR'S
KISS

PLUTARCH, *LIVES*, 'ALEXANDER'

After sailing with his fleet on an expedition through difficult terrain, Plutarch tells us that Alexander the Great's infantry suffered from diseases, famine and the parching sun. They spent sixty days in miserable conditions, but eventually reached Gedrosia – the Greek name for the region now known as Makran, on the coast of the Gulf of Oman – where they were given everything they needed in abundance, and were provided for by princes.

Bagoas was a eunuch in the court of the Persian Empire. According to one Roman historian, Quintus Curtius Rufus, Bagoas won the favour of Alexander the Great through prostitution, having 'made a female of himself'. In Plutarch's *Lives*, Alexander is depicted as warm and fiery, but also as a man with much self-control, particularly over 'the pleasures of the body', making the following account even more unusual and touching, a return of festivity and tenderness after the perils of an expedition.

After taking a rest, Alexander set out with his forces and marched for seven days through Carmania, and it wasn't long before the march turned into a sort of bacchanal, full of drinking and dancing. There wasn't a shield or a sword to be seen: instead, the sun glinted on skin, and the soldiers dipped great horns and cups into casks of wine, and the land around them resounded with music.

Alexander feasted all day and all night, laying himself down with his companions on a dais pulled by eight horses. Some of the men followed the royal float in wagons draped

with purple canopies and embroidered cloths. There were
vehicles shaded with great branches full of green leaves,
and under the leaves there were dappled throngs of soldiers,
drunk, with flower-crowns on their heads.

By the waysides, men stumbled, dazed by the drink and
the sun, and toasted one another. And it wasn't just drinking
– there was raucous music and dancing and the moving
bronze of bare skin. It was as though the god himself were
there, leading the revels. Then, when the troupe arrived
at the palace of Gedrosia, the army passed out, exhausted,
and Alexander began celebrating another festival.

One day, when he was drunk, he went to watch a contest,
and saw his favourite – Bagoas – among the dancers, and
Bagoas won the prize. Afterwards, Bagoas walked across
the theatre, still in his dancing costume, wearing his new
crown, and he sat beside Alexander. The crowd cheered
and applauded him, and called for the king to kiss the
winner. Finally, Alexander agreed; and with a smile on his
face, he pulled Bagoas into his arms and kissed him tenderly.

A LOVER'S
MONUMENT

PAUSANIAS, *DESCRIPTION OF GREECE*

In this short topographical passage, the geographer and traveller Pausanias draws his readers' attention to a small tomb, a landmark, which holds the body of Sostratus, the beloved of Heracles (also known by the Greek equivalent Hercules). The passage shows us how queer tales were immortalized physically in the ancient world. But there is also something moving in the briefness of the remark here. No undue attention is given to this hero by the writer. Sostratus is not, as we might say now, tokenized. Rather, he is remembered among all the other landmarks – the statues and the rivers and the temples – as an equal among the histories and the heroes of the region. His story is given in a straightforward tone; the grief of Heracles is related in much the same way as the grief of any partner for their beloved. This normality, in its own way, is touching: it shows us, in the eyes of the writer and his readers, the beautiful ordinariness of this love.

The river Larisus marks the boundary between Achaia and Elis, and by the river there sits a temple to Athena. About thirty stades from there is Dyme, an Achaean city. Dyme was the only Achaean city that Philip, Demetrius' son, subjugated in the wars. It was sacked by soldiers afterwards, and later annexed by Augustus to the city of Patras.

In ancient times, before the Ionians changed it, the name of the city was Paleia. I'm not sure if Dyme comes from the name of a local woman, or from Dymas, who was the son of Aegimius. Either way, no one should fall for the inscription on the statue of Oebotas at Olympia. Oebotas, who came from this city, and won a great race, was honoured with this monument, and the words on it say that

Oebotas, an Achaean, and son of Oenias, won a foot-race
And increased the honour of his fatherland, Paleia

But the Greek poets were always using ancient names rather than modern ones, and at the time the city was named Dyme rather than Paleia.

Anyway, just before you get to this city, on the right-hand side of the road, you'll see the grave of Sostratus. He came from the city, and was the beloved of Heracles, who outlived him and built a tomb for the young man, cutting an offering of hair from his own head as a symbol of grief and piety. Even now, if you visit the grave, you'll see a figure of Heracles cut into the surface of the main slab. I'm told the local people still make sacrifices to Sostratus, who is remembered as a hero in the city.

HERACLES
& HYLAS

THEOCRITUS, *IDYLLS*

One of the most enduring and popular of the Greek myths, the tale of Heracles and Hylas – two Argonauts accompanying Jason on his mission to steal the Golden Fleece – is featured throughout Western art. John William Waterhouse's painting *Hylas and the Nymphs* (1896) shows a scene of close erotic temptation between the young Hylas and the nude deities draped in waterweeds and lilies, and the tale has been used by queer writers like Christopher Marlowe and Oscar Wilde as an archetypal image of mourning.

Told in a frame, wherein Theocritus relates the story to his partner, Nicias, the poem shows us how queer myths become central texts to relationships outside of mythic time. In the 'present moment' of the passage, Theocritus and his lover reflect on the story of Heracles and Hylas, and so the poem sets up possible parallels, where the story Theocritus is telling becomes a sort of model of queer love for him and his lover. In this way, we are not the only audience for the story: Nicias, Theocritus' lover, hears it with us. It is a story full of lush sadness. The tragic scene of Theocritus' Idyll, in which Heracles calls in search of Hylas, and Hylas tries to respond from beneath the water, is heart-wrenching in its dual perspectives. One on level, there is Heracles' point of view; but as a reader, we see the tale from above, witnessing both the desperate lover, driven to grief by searching, and the lost beloved, hidden just out of sight.

When Love came to us, from wherever it sprang,
we believed, Nicias, that he was born for us alone.
But how could we think it? Love has come to others,
he has made all things beautiful to eyes not ours.
After all, Amphitryon's brave son, whose heart

seemed cased in bronze, could hold his own
against a savage lion, but not against a boy.
He too once loved a lad: beautiful Hylas,
with his long curls of hair still uncut. Just as a father
would to a son, he taught the boy all he knew,
but gently, though he himself had learned
life's lessons the hard way. He never left Hylas' side:
not when day rose to noon, nor when dawn
drove her white horses against the night
and neither when the mother-hen gathered
her brood into the smoky roost to sleep.
He gave himself as an example to the boy,
so that Hylas might be fashioned into the best
of men. So when Jason, son of Aeson, sailed out
in search of the Golden Fleece, and the finest

were chosen from the finest cities in the land,
the hero chose Hylas to accompany him
on the *Argo*. Early on, the ship sheared through the sea,
gliding unscathed through the rough waters.
It swept like an eagle into the calm gulf of Phasis.

Then, at the rising of the Pleiades, when the signs
of the summer season bloomed everywhere,
the band of men were again eager for voyaging.
They each took their place in the hollow of the *Argo*
and set sail for the Hellespont. In three days' time,
the fine winds had guided them to anchor
in Propontis, in sight of the fertile lands, where oxen
pulled the soil into bright, smooth furrows.
They disembarked the ship, thinking
of their evening meal; but first they made a bed
among the meadow-straw – one mattress
of flowers and grasses for them all, stitched
from the blades of galingale and of rushes.
Meanwhile, golden-haired Hylas was wandering
through the cool dusk, carrying in his hands
a vessel to fetch back water for the camp,
for Heracles and for Telamon. Before long, he saw
a spring, sunken down in a valley cleft, thick
with blue swallow-wort, maidenhair and parsley.
Under the surface, in the pool, there were nymphs
dancing. Like water, nymphs never rest. And when Hylas
leant down to the spring, and dipped the pitcher's
mouth beneath the lip of the water, their hands
grasped him. They took him by the wrist, the clarity
of their thought disturbed and shocked
by the suddenness of their desire. Hylas called out

as he crashed through the surface of the pool.
Like a searing star that shoots its light
across the midnight sea, and seems to fall
into it, so that a mariner might say 'Loosen the ropes,
lads; there's a wind afoot', so Hylas
with the light of his golden hair fell
through the water. He struggled, and cried,
and the nymphs stretched his taut body
across them, and spoke gently in his ear.

It wasn't long before Heracles began to worry
at the boy's absence, and went out
in search of him, carrying his bow and cudgel.
He cried out loudly to Hylas three times
in his deep voice, and Hylas cried back three times
from under the water, desperate to be heard.
As when a bleating fawn cries in the echoing hills,
and a lion sets out in search of it, so Heracles
went wildly through the briars and the weeds,
back and forth, torn apart with grief. Through fields,
through woods, he punished himself for love,
fearing his own failure, and all thoughts of Jason
and the *Argo* vanished. The night passed,
and as dawn came the ship raised its tackle
and the crew stood waiting for Heracles' return,
but the man had driven himself wild
filling the woods and the valleys with Hylas' name.
Now, the golden-haired boy lives, never fading,
amid immortal company, and Heracles, by the men,
was shunned for desertion. But it was not so:
he finished the journey alone, and came on foot
at last to the bleak land of the Colchians.

DON'T FEED
THE HORSES

PHILOSTRATUS THE ELDER, *IMAGES*

This passage attests to the violence and savagery of martial heroism. It describes the eighth of the Twelve Labours of Heracles, in which he is sent by King Eurystheus to steal the mares of Diomedes – flesh-eating, wild and mad creatures chained by iron fastenings to a bronze manger. In this version of the story, Heracles' companion, Abderus, is left in charge of the horses, and is eaten alive. In revenge, Heracles feeds Diomedes to the mares, and slays them, before stealing back the body of Abderus for burial. It is a passage full of carnage and bloodshed, out of which arises the image of the grief-stricken hero carrying the mangled body of his beloved.

Listen. It would hardly be fair to think that the mares
of Diomedes were a labour for Heracles: he has defeated them
already, he has battered them to the ground with his club.
See, the bloodied body of one lies there; another is gasping
for its last breaths; one is leaping, the other falling down.
They are knotted and unkempt, their manes torn and shaggy.
No better than wild beasts. See, their stalls are stained
with the blood and the torn muscle of the men Diomedes
fed to them. And their breeder? Even more savage
than the animals he has fallen beside. Still, this task
is doubled in difficulty: Eros has brought it to Heracles
alongside his other labours. It's no small thing. Right now, look:
Heracles is bearing the half-eaten body of Abderus,
wrenched from the mouths of the horses. He was so young,
poor lad. Younger than Iphitus. See, the skin that is left

on his bones is smooth and unworn and still beautiful.
The tears Heracles sheds, the close embrace of the men,
the grief etched into the hero's exhausted face –
if only these could be taken by another, if only another
could go beneath the monument on Abderus' tomb.
O, let it bear another's name. But no grave is enough
for Heracles, no tomb can hold his mourning and so,
sweet hero, he will build a city for Abderus, his love,
and call it by his name, and sports will be instituted
in his honour; and, excepting the equestrian, the city
will celebrate all contests in his memory.

IPHIS & IANTHE

OVID, *METAMORPHOSES*

In Ovid's *Metamorphoses*, the story of Iphis and Ianthe comes immediately after the story of Byblis, who falls in love with her twin brother, Caunus, and, distraught at being rejected by him, is changed into a spring. Moving once more into the private world of the family home, Ovid relates another tale. A couple of middle-to-low income cannot afford to support a female child, and the husband resolves that, if his wife gives birth to a daughter, the girl must be killed. The mother, Telethúsa, gives birth to a daughter, Iphis, who is spared from death by being raised as a boy. Trouble comes when Iphis is promised in marriage to a beautiful girl named Ianthe.

This is a tale of the forbidden desire between women, but the story of Iphis and Ianthe is hardly a celebration. In fact, when love between the two develops, Iphis is racked with shame, finding no correlation in the natural world for her desire. Many readers will no doubt find resonances here: in Iphis' desperate denial, her turmoil, her lonely desire to be otherwise. In the end, the intervention of the god Isis delivers Iphis and her mother from their secret shame. Perhaps, in a world set against her desire, the transfiguration was merciful. Still, it is hard not to read a sombre undercurrent in this tale of a woman in love with another woman, who must be utterly changed in order to conform.

The tale of Byblis' metamorphosis would perhaps have spread
through the Cretan cities had the island not also heard
of another miracle closer to home: the disturbance of Iphis' change.
It was a long time ago, in the region of Phaestos, not far
from Knossos, that a man of little fame lived. His name was Ligdus,
a free-born man, though one of the people, with no more money
than might be expected of a man of his lowly birth. Still,
he was an honest man, and well-respected. His wife, Telethúsa,

was pregnant, and it was nearing the time of the birth
when Ligdus sat her down, and gave her a warning: 'My prayers,'
he said, 'are twofold: firstly, I pray that your labour is easy,
that you are safe; and secondly, that the child will be a boy.
We cannot afford to keep a girl, Telethúsa. They are trouble,
and have no strength. So if (have mercy) the child is female,
we must put her to death.' He asked forgiveness for uttering
his thought, and cried as he said it, and the mother cried too,
both of them in equal measure. Telethúsa begged her husband
not to hold her to that prayer, but her words were wasted –
his mind could not be changed. And so, when her waters
moved, and the child grew too heavy to be carried
inside her, the mother prayed at night, prayed inside
a dream, and in the dream Isis came to her. The god
was standing at the foot of the bed with all her sacred
wardens at her side. Isis had horns like crescent moons
on her brow. She had a wheaten garland sewn with gold
around her head. She came with Anubis, with the dog's head,
and Bubastis, and Apis, the bull with the dappled hide,
and another god who raised a finger to its lips, commanding
silence. Osiris was there too, and the Egyptian serpent,
swollen with soporific venom. Telethúsa felt wide awake,
and saw everything clear as day when Isis spoke to her: 'Telethúsa,
I have come to you, one of my devoted worshippers. Put away
your cares and sorrows. Ignore your husband's orders.
When your child is delivered, do not be afraid to raise it,
no matter the sex. I am the goddess who comes to aid
the ones who appeal to me. Let it never be said that those
who worship me go unrewarded.' Speaking those lines,
Isis passed from the chamber, and Telethúsa rose from her bed,
lifted her hands in supplication to the stars, and prayed
that the dream was real.

When, finally, the woman
went into labour, her child came quickly, and entered
the world as a girl, though the secret was kept
from her father. The mother told everyone
to keep good care of her boy, and the pretence
was upheld, because only the nurse knew the truth.
When Ligdus, the father, had said his vows to the gods,
he lifted the child up and pronounced his name: *Iphis*.
It was the name of his grandfather, and the mother
rejoiced. You see, Iphis was a name common
among both boys and girls, and she could use it
without deceit. So it was that the falsehood, which began
through the protection of the mother, was upheld.
The child was dressed as a boy, and its face
gave nothing away: it would have been beautiful
on any body.

Thirteen years passed by, and then,
Iphis' father found her a bride in golden-haired Ianthe.
The girl was praised among all the women of Phaestos
for her beauty, and the two were equal in age and charm,
having learned about the world from the same teacher
in their youth. So too, when it came, their love for each other
was equal: their hearts both burned with an equal fire,
but their hopes in love were not equal. Ianthe, the lovely girl,
dreamed sweetly of the night they would be married,
and believed that this man, Iphis, would be her husband.
But Iphis' love was riddled with doubt and fear, and grew
all the more fervent because of it, passing beyond reason –
she was, in this way, like any girl madly in love with another.
One evening, scarcely able to hold back her tears, she sighed:
'O, what will all this come to? What will happen to me?

A love possesses me that I have no language for, that no one
has ever spoken of, or heard of, before. It is monstrous
and unmatched, this desire. If the gods wanted to spare me,
they should have done it. Or if they wanted to ruin me,
they should have ruined me with some natural affliction.
Cows do not love cows; mares do not love mares. Instead,
the ram lusts for the sheep, and the stag pursues the doe.
Just so, the birds make love. In the whole world of animals
I cannot think of a time when one girl has loved another.
O gods, I wish I were not a woman at all! But this island
I live on … Crete is the home of every perversion. It produces
all sorts of monstrous things. Didn't Pasiphaë lust after a bull?
But then, the bull was male … It's useless. My passions are wilder
even than that. Even Pasiphaë had some hope of fulfilment.
Gods, even if all the ingenuity of the world should cluster here,
even if Dedalus himself returned to Crete on his waxen wings,
what could he do? With all the art of the world, and of history,
could he change me into a boy? Could he change you, Ianthe?'

   The girl took hold of herself. 'Stop it, Iphis. Be brave.
Shake off this reckless love. Get free of it. Remember
your body: you were born a woman. Have you deceived yourself
like you have deceived others? You must be moral, you must love
as a woman ought to love. See, it is hope that keeps love alive,
and your love for Ianthe is hopeless. No guardian stands
between you, no jealous husband, no cruel father; and Ianthe
herself loves you. Still, you cannot have her.' Iphis shook herself
punishingly. 'None of my prayers have been denied. The gods,
lovingly, have given me what was theirs to give. What I wish
my father also wishes; likewise, what Ianthe's father wishes,
so does Ianthe. But it is nature who rejects us; nature
who roots inside me and causes my distress, and now

the wedding day is at hand, and soon Ianthe will be mine
and yet not mine. There will be water everywhere, and still
I will thirst. O Juno, O Hymen – why are you presiding
over a wedding where there are two brides, and no groom?'

With those words, she broke off. Meanwhile, Ianthe
was in her own turmoil. She too was praying, but her prayer
was to hasten Hymen to the nuptials. Her longing
was matched only by its inverse, that of the troubled mind
of Telethúsa, the mother of Iphis, who was desperately
playing for time, postponing the wedding, inventing all sorts
of illnesses and omens and prophetic, menacing dreams.
Soon, she had burned through all manner of excuses
and exhausted each one. The time for lighting torches
had come. Only a day remained before the wedding.

The mother and daughter unloosed their hair, and clung
to the altar of Isis, their ringlets splayed across their faces.
'Goddess who haunts Paraetonium, who haunts the Mareotic Lake,
who pervades Pharos and the seven waters of the Nile,
help us, come to us now, the hour of our need is here.
It was long ago that I saw you last, in a dream – I knew you,
all your emblems and your wardens. I heard the clashing
of the sistra. And didn't I store your words in my mind?
Didn't I note your commands? It was your gift, your wisdom,
that helped my child live, that hid us from my husband's rage.
Pity us, Isis, both of us – help us now when we need you.'
Telethúsa wept wildly as she prayed. Then: something stirred.
The altar of the goddess began to shudder and tremble.
The doors shook on their hinges, and the horns of the statue
of Isis seemed to shoot out beams of light. Listen!
Even the sistra, the goddess's tambourine, began to chime.
Still anxious, the mother clung in her mind to the omen.
She left the temple, and Iphis walked beside her. Strange,
how the daughter's stride seemed longer now. Strange,
how her face was a darker hue. And odd, very odd, the way
her features seemed to have sharpened. Even the locks
of her hair, loosed in curls, were shorter than before.
There was a new vigour to her … Suddenly, it dawned:
Iphis, who was once a girl, was now a boy. O, go Iphis!
Go and shower the shrines with offerings! Be glad.
The mother and child ran happily to show their joy,
and placed a votive tablet at a shrine, inscribed
with these words: *These gifts Iphis paid as a man*
which once as a girl he promised. So, when the morning sun
unveiled the wide world with its light, and Venus,
Juno and Hymen gathered by the marriage fires,
the boy Iphis arrived to marry his beloved Ianthe.

SOPHIA'S SPELL

SUPPLEMENTUM MAGICUM

This 'binding spell' from the *Supplementum Magicum*, dating from the third or fourth century AD, was found in Egypt, and is full of passionate desire. The text, written on a lead tablet, attests to the power of female same-sex love in Roman Egypt, and is full of untranslatable magic language. A woman named Sophia calls up a variety of underworld deities to inflame the liver of another woman, Gorgonia, with love for her. The magic words – or *voces magicae* – are unintelligible, but are meant to signify the power of the spell and the names of the conjured demons. It is a heady, intense and dramatic hex; full of a throbbing will to power and domination, wherein Gorgonia will be 'enslaved' to Sophia. This language, which according to scholar Lucy Parr is common in heterosexual erotic spells of the time, overflows with violence and the rhythmic patterning of a dark sorcery. The spell begins by invoking Cerberus, the three-headed dog who guards the gates of the underworld.

Beneath the firmament, in the tar-black dark, O vicious-
toothed Cerberus, coiled in snakes, your three heads are
turning. O traveller in the uncharted territories of the
afterworld, come. Come out with the Furies, those savage
women with their stinging whips, with their serpent hair.
Rise up, rise up as I summon you. Before I use this
incantation to force and persuade you, turn out a fire-
breathing demon. Listen, listen to me, and act quickly:
do not oppose me. You are the governors of the Earth.

*Alalachos allēch Harmachimeneus magimeneus athinembēs
astazabathos artazabathos ōkoum phlom Ionchachinachana* thou
Azael and Lykael and Beliam and Belenea and *sochosocham
somochan sozocham ouzacham bauzacham oueddouch*

O corpse-demon, conjured up from the deep, inflame the
heart and liver and spirit of Gorgonia, daughter of Nilogenia:
spike it with love and longing for Sophia, daughter of
Isara. Hold Gorgonia down: restrain her: make her fling
herself into the bathhouse for Sophia, daughter of Isara,
and you, corpse-demon, turn yourself into a bath woman
to stoke the fires. Burn her, set her soul alight, strike
a light on her heart, her liver, her spirit and watch them
sear with heat. Drive Gorgonia, daughter of Nilogenia,
to torment and never let it rest: day and night, night and
day, force her through the streets and through the houses
in lust for Sophia, in love for her: let her submit like
a slave, let her hand over all her possessions to Sophia,
let the gods command it!

iartana ousousio ipsenthanchochainchoueoch aeeioyo iartana ousiou-
siou ipsoenpeuthadei | annoucheo aeeioyo

Holy lord of the afterlife, holding the sceptre of Tartaros
and the sceptre of Styx and the sceptre of murderous Lethe,
look: even the hairs on Cerberus' back stand up in fear of
you. Crack the whips of the Erinyes. I know how soft the
couch of Persephone is when you lie upon it, how it soothes
you. Whether you are Sarapis, who all the firmament
trembles before, or Osiris, star of Egypt, your minion is the
all-knowing boy; and Anubis, wonderous herald of the dead,
is yours. Come, come out, and aid me: I am summoning you
with occult and terrible symbols:

achaipho thotho aie aie ai ai eia othoth ophiacha emen barasthrom-
ouai monsymphiris tophammieartheiaeaima saaooeuase enberouba
amen ouralis sothalis sothe mou raktrasimour achorame chreimier
moithips thabapsrabou thilbarphix | zameneth zatarata

kyphartanna anne Ereschigal eplangarbothithoea diadax sothara
sierseir symmytha phrennobatha oae – leichoiretakestreu ioxeiarneu
koryneuknyoro alis sotheoth dodekakiste, swallowing the tip of
the tail, *sok – roume souchiar anoch anoch brittandra skylm –*
achal bathrael amabrima chremla aostrachin amou salenasau tat
chola sorsangar madoure | boasaraoul saroucha sisiro zacharro ibibi
barbal sobouch Osir ouoai Azel abadaot – iobadaon berbaiso chio
yyy phthobal lamach chamarchoth basar batharar neaipeschioth
– phorphor iyzze yze chych chych

Hold Gorgonia, daughter of Nilogenia: make her cast
herself down into the bathhouse. Make her do it for

Sophia, daughter of Isara. For her alone. Yes, chthonic king, burn, burn, and ignite, inflame her heart, her liver, her spirit, with love and desire for me. Drive her mad for me. Torment her constantly. Force her running through the streets and houses. Enslave her to Sophia. Let her give up all she possesses. Let her give up herself. O terrible demon of the underworld, read the spell on this tablet and translate it into action.

> *Thobarabau Semeseilamps sasibel sarephtho Iao ieou ia thyeoeo aeeioyo panchouchi thassautho Soth Phre ipechenbor Sesengen Barpharagges olam boro sepansase thobaustho iaphthp sou thoou*

I incant it again: do not deny my desires: throw her into the bathhouse for Sophia's sake: burn, burn, ignite, set on fire her heart, her liver, her spirit: this is the will of God.

> *achor achor achchach ptoumi chachcho charachoch chaptoume characharachor aptoumi mechochaptou charachptou chachacho characho otenachocheu* and *sissiro sisi phermou Chmouor Harouer Abrasaz Phnounoboel ochloba zarachoa barichamo* who is called *bacham kehk*

Force her to cast herself into the bathhouse, and stoke the fires. Make Gorgonia love Sophia passionately, unquenchably, tortuously, unceasingly. O Sun, honey-holder, honey-maker, O drive her into the inferno of the spirits: make her mine: destroy: torment: enflame: give her wholly to me.

A FIELD
OF KISSES

CATULLUS, 48

The poet Catullus is a writer of many moods. His poems, which
are mostly short, are famed for their beautiful, sonorous forms
and, often, for their direct treatments of love, and what readers
might think of as their obscenity. Here, he addresses a sensual
and romantic poem to Juventius, one of his male lovers. What
I love about this lyric is its keen sense of the interplay between
abundance and satisfaction. Rather than desiring what is rare,
or seeing love as a finite commodity, here the imagery is one of
plenty: sun-ripened fields in harvest time. Though the poem
tries to count kisses, it realizes between the lines that kisses
cannot be counted as coins or hours can. The more we kiss,
Catullus seems to say, the more kisses we make. The more we
kiss, the more kisses we want.

Steeped in honey, Juventius,
your golden eyes, and as sweet too
when I press my lips to them –
three hundred thousand kisses
is not close to enough. Even if I plucked
each kiss like an amber grain
from a ripe, sun-warmed field
in late summer – sheaves
and sheaves of them – my love,
it would not be enough.

FURIUS
& AURELIUS

CATULLUS, 16

In Catullus' poem 15, he addresses Aurelius, entrusting the man with the thing he loves most, 'his boy'. Catullus tells Aurelius to protect the boy, and not to have sex with him. 'You can wave your erection anywhere you like,' he says, 'but not at my boy.' In a particularly gruesome threat, the poet says that, if Aurelius defies him, he will chain his feet together and push radishes and mullet fins into 'the open door' of Aurelius' anus. This poem, also referred to as poem 16, finds Catullus again in vengeful throes, directing his anger at two lovers, Aurelius and Furius, who have accused Catullus the man of being as licentious as his own poems.

I'll have you gagging, I'll bend you over,
Furius and Aurelius, you pig and breeder,
if you think I'm as obscene as my poems.
A poet can be filthy in his lines and pure
in life. So what if I throw in some heat,
some sweat and spice to get some hairy
old men hard? Do 'a thousand kisses'
and 'sweet lips' make me less of a man?
Come here. Say it again. I'll show you
what a man is when I plough your holes
and fuck your faces up.

PHILAENIS' EXPLOITS

MARTIAL, *EPIGRAMS*

Martial's 'obscene' epigrams were often seen as too risqué to translate into English. If you were to look up two of these epigrams in the Loeb Classical Library edition (1919), or the Bohn's Classic Library edition (1897), you would be met with a blank space.

Here, Martial describes Philaenis – an androgynous woman who has an appetite for dominating boys and girls. Despite the tone of disgust, the poems present images of queer women so powerful, so contrary, as to confound the heterosexual gaze altogether.

Philaenis, the king-dyke, buggers boys.
She's hornier than a married man.
She fucks nearly a dozen girls a day.
She rolls up her skirts and throws herself
into manly sports; smears grit
over herself and wrestles. She joins the gays
swinging their dumbbells round;
garners a stench of sweat; and then
afterwards, downs her booze
and vomits it up just in time
for dinner, where she scoffs sixteen
training rations and washes them down
with a burp. Then, strong and steady,
she's ready to fuck. She won't suck cock –
that's for sissies. No – she plunges
her tongue into the cracks of women.
Philaenis, king of the dykes, may the gods
give you all your butch heart desires.

TRIBADE OF TRIBADES

MARTIAL, *EPIGRAMS*

Here, in this brief epigram, we meet Philaenis again. The tone has shifted to reverence. Philaenis is unrepentant, unashamed, and we seem encouraged to stand in awe of her power and natural supremacy.

Queen of queens, most powerful of the pussy-lovers:
Philaenis, it's only right that you call the woman you fuck
your girlfriend.

BASSA ISN'T INTO YOU

MARTIAL, *EPIGRAMS*

Finally, we meet Bassa, who rebuffs the gaze of the male speaker, consorting only with other women. There's a sense of profound irritation here, of chastisement, and also a wonderful feeling of defiance in the fact that Bassa seems to ignore (or at least, doesn't answer) the speaker's jibes. Bassa isn't into men, and she's certainly not going to waste her time with this pestering poet.

Still, Bassa, I never saw you kiss a man,
and none of your fancy talk ever won you one –
for every question you found the answer
in your own kind – and no man came close.
You seemed to me like the perfect wife, but –
and how outrageous – you fucked women.
Bassa, you had the nerve to rub your pussy
against another; to play up a penis with a toy.
You've made a mighty riddle, Bassa.
The Sphinx would be proud of you. Here,
though no man is around, adultery
is everywhere.

SAPPHO
& ATTHIS

Sappho's poems were written to be sung to the accompaniment of music. Though most are lost, she was and remains one of the most highly regarded poets of antiquity. Heralding from the island of Lesbos, her love-filled verses have become touchstones of lesbian identity. In these texts, we can see the fragmentary nature of her surviving poems, and also the sensuous descriptive powers of her writing. Here, an unnamed Lydian woman remembers a person called Atthis, who is likely to be the 'you' that the poem is addressed to. The gaps seem to mirror the distraction of love, the glimpsed images and memories that fill a mind lost in longing.

in Sardis …
often holding her thoughts here …

you, you were like a goddess to her,
more than any others, your songs

delighted her … Now she goes
among Lydian women, shining,

just as the moon with her gentle beams
outshines all the stars of the firmament

when the sun sinks down … Equal, her light
over the meadows, the salt sea; the roses

unfurling in the dew, and the chervil
and the sweet clover jewelled with it …

So she wanders there, longing for Atthis,
her gentle mind eaten by the past …

WATCHING YOU WITHOUT ME

SAPPHO, 31

Fragment 31 is one of Sappho's best-known poems. In it, the speaker watches a young woman being caressed by a man, and expresses her intense desire to take the man's place. The poem gives a sense of distance, of sensuous longing, and of the separation that, rather than extinguishing love, raises it to an unbearable intensity. There is a gorgeous attention to the bodily sensation of jealousy here – the fire prickling under the skin, the sense of dread – all framed in the startlingly recognizable image of watching, from across the room, an unrequited love talking to someone else.

That man looks like a god descended,
the one pressed to you, his face in yours,
your breaths together in the sweet talk
and laughter of your embrace …

It makes my heart flutter, my chest
uneasy to watch the two of you.
I try to speak, but my voice
is lost with the sight of you.

There is a fire, a gauze of flame
flickering under my skin, and my vision
hazes, blurs, and I hear the thunder
of my own heart beating in my ears,

and I find I have turned pale,
sallow as the grass, almost on the edge
of death as I watch, and know
I must stay here, feeling always so …

APOLLO &
CYPARISSUS

OVID, *METAMORPHOSES*

In this short tale, we meet Cyparissus, a beautiful young man from the island of Ceos. Beloved of Apollo, Cyparissus is himself enamoured with a stag who is treasured by the nymphs of Carthaea, one of the four Ancient Greek city-states on the island. The stag is tame, and is decorated with precious jewels. One day, in a tragic accident, Cyparissus throws his javelin and kills the stag. Apollo, out of mercy, transforms the youth into a cypress tree – traditionally associated with mourning and the underworld.

Among the woods:
there is a cypress tree, conical, like a marker
on a race-track showing the turn. But no –
that tree was a boy once, a boy loved by the god
who tunes the lyre and strings the bow.

Once, there was a heavy stag, sacred to the nymphs
who haunted the fields of Carthaea. This stag
had wide antlers. They branched so far that they cast
a shadow across its head. They shone with gold,
and the stag wore on its neck a collar of jewels.
A silver ball, like a charm, quivered on the stag's brow
and bronze pearls hung by his hollow temples.
Now, this stag was free from fear, and had forgotten
the shyness of his nature. He used to visit people
at their homes, and would stretch his neck
to be stroked. And to you, Cyparissus –
most beautiful of the Cean boys – he was dear

above all others. You led the stag to green fields
and to springs of clear water. You would weave
the wildflowers through his horns. Sometimes,
like a horseman, you'd climb up on his back
and journey with him, guiding him lightly
with purple reins.

             It was noon, one summer's day,
when the claws of Cancer were burning in the sun.
The weary stag was resting on the shaded grass
by the cool of a woodland. And Cyparissus,
the handsome boy, was playing, and threw
his javelin in the air and, by accident, speared it –
and when he saw the death-wound, and heard
the stag crying out, he longed to die beside it.
There was no soothing word that bright Apollo
did not say to the boy, no solace he did not whisper
into his ear, but Cyparissus could not be calmed –
he sighed and begged and grieved, asking
that the gods let him mourn for ever, and his tears
flowed in such profusion that his blood
was used up, and his limbs began to shift
in colour, becoming green, and his hair –
which had hung over his pale brow – bristled
into a crown, and Cyparissus stiffened upwards
into a spiked crest, pointing to the heavens.
And Apollo grieved for him, and sighed, and said:

'I will mourn for you for ever, and you
will mourn for others too, and enter
into the language of their sorrows.'

ALFENUS, MY FORSAKER

CATULLUS, 30

There's a sense of utter abandonment in this poem. Catullus appears as a lover who has been dumped, cast off like an old coat. Having been betrayed, he has lost all sense of trust in the world. It's not long, though, before the spikier side of Catullus' voice returns: trusting to a sort of divine justice, he warns his ex-lover that it won't be long before he'll get a taste of his own medicine.

Alfenus, my forsaker, fickle in friendship
to comrades and lovers alike – have you forgotten me?
Was it so easy to throw off my love like an old coat?
Ah, the gods in the heavens are watching, Alfenus,
and you have left me fallen, you have walked away.
Is there nothing a man can trust? No faith
in friendship? Once, you drew me out of myself –
ribboned my soul into yours, unspooled my cares
in your hands. But now, with you letting go, the winds
have blown all of me away. Everything is lost,
all those days hurried into the clouds. But the gods,
from your ways, have made a seed. Soon, they will crop
its bitter herb, and give it to you to taste.

A PRAYER,
OF SORTS

CATULLUS, 50

It's a relief to meet Catullus again in a romantic, tender frame
of mind. Here, rather than being abandoned, he's at the very
beginning of love, full of possibility and a sweet, exciting anxiety.
The poem itself is a memento and a plea, supposedly left for
Licinius to find. Catullus is daring to hope, to love again, and
wants his Licinius to know how precious a heart is, how rare
a thing new love is, and how easily startled it is in its early days.

It was only yesterday, Licinius,
in our idle hours, that we played
at poetry – switching metres, testing
form and music on the air, conjuring
our images from the wine. I left
aflame, radiant with your face, your wit –
I lay down that night, but could not sleep.
I turned and turned in the dark and longed
for light, for morning, for you. God,
I sweated. I saw visions of your face.
I heard you speaking. In bed, I made
this poem for you – a testament,
a record of our bliss, my longing.
Do not toss it out, Licinius, apple
of my eye. It is a prayer, of sorts;
and Nemesis is waiting, night
and day for you – for us – to mess it up.

ON DESIRE

LUCRETIUS, *ON THE NATURE OF THINGS*

Lucretius' epic poem *On the Nature of Things* is a vast and strange book, ranging through subjects such as earthquakes, metallurgy and the soul. If there is no afterlife, and no divine intervention, Lucretius suggests that the principal object of life is pleasure.

Just before this passage, Lucretius has been thinking about the imagination, and how it responds to the world when we sleep. Though others might think of dreams as prophecies, Lucretius thinks of them in a very modern way, as places to play, to explore, and to act out our desires. From here, he moves daringly into the subject of wet dreams, thinking about how the mind goes off in search of pleasure even when we are asleep. The language moves beautifully between the anatomical and the philosophical, giving a richness that draws out the mysteries of the body, of the mind, and of love.

It arrives when adolescence comes
and strengthens the body; the seed
wakening in us, stirring the limbs,
and some present or remembered image
of another person invades the mind, bringing
the look of a lovely face, the human scent –
young boys are visited by dreams
of those images each night, and brought
to a point of heat, so the seed
(as though the act had been achieved)
bursts through them and floods
across their sheets. The seed,
as I say, is stimulated when a boy
comes of age and feels impulses

he didn't know before. Only
another person can draw them out.
It starts across the body, then moves
through the limbs, the organs,
until it swells between his legs and lifts
the penis up – and the boy can't help
but desire to expel it into the person
who roused it. His mind is wounded
by love, and yearns for the one
who dealt the blow, just as a soldier
falls in the direction of the wounding sword
or a gash spurts blood towards its inflictor.
So, someone pierced with the dart
of Venus – whether by a boy with svelte
and girlish limbs, or by a woman – turns
to the source of his hurt, and longs
for union, longs to shoot his seed.
The images of desire are urgent
and sweet. Though they are wordless,
they speak of many joys to come.

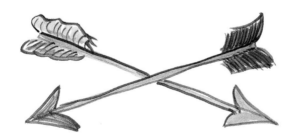

BETRAYAL
IN THE
BATHHOUSE

PETRONIUS, *THE SATYRICON*

The Satyricon (late first century AD) – a work of Latin fiction sometimes described as a novel, and written in a mixture of prose and verse – follows the strange, sometimes disturbing and always outrageous adventures of the narrator, Encolpius, and his handsome sixteen-year-old slave and boyfriend, Giton.

What is particularly notable about the work is the way that Petronius blends satire and sentimentality, threading together romance and brutal humour. That blend is showcased brilliantly here, where betrayal and fickleness are undercut by a poignant regret. Just before the following episode, Giton is seduced by another man, Ascyltus; and on being discovered by Encolpius, he has decided to stay with his seducer. After spending some days apart, Encolpius turns surly, and sets out with a sword to avenge himself. Eventually he is disarmed, and is sidetracked by entering a picture gallery, but as he is returning home in the company of an old poet named Eumolpus, he bumps into Giton. What follows is a tale of adultery, reconciliation and then the pain of remembering.

I saw Giton, with some towels and some brushes, leaning against the wall, looking sad and embarrassed. You could tell he was uncomfortable and dejected, being a slave. When he turned towards me, catching my eye, his face softened with pleasure, and he said:

'Forgive me, brother. Look, there are no weapons here, no threats, so I can speak freely. Take me with you, away from this savage criminal. You can punish me however you like. I'm full of regret, and it would ease my mind to know that, if I died, it was at your hand, and because you willed it.'

I told him to keep quiet in case someone should hear our plans. We left Eumolpus behind – he was reciting a poem in the bathhouse – and I dragged Giton out by a dank, shadowed exit and flew with him straight to my lodgings. Then, once the doors were barred, I pulled him close to me, and rubbed my face against his cheek, which was wet with tears. For a long time neither of us could speak. My boy's handsome body was heaving with sobs.

'It's shameful, and a wonder,' I said, 'that, even though you deserted me, I still love you. Somehow, there is no scar left on my heart, where before there was a great wound. Explain yourself! What did I do to deserve it? Why did you give yourself to a stranger?'

When he heard those words, and realized I still loved him, he raised his eyes to mine. I carried on speaking. 'I left the choice at your doors. I left my love in your hands. But I will never say another thing, I will never bring it up again, if you prove your love by keeping your word.'

I said all this through tears, and he wiped them gently with his cloak, and said:

'Now, now, Encolpius, turn again to your memory, and question it. Did I leave you, or did you betray me? I'm not ashamed to admit one thing – that when I saw two armed men before me, I chose the side of the stronger.'

I pressed my lips to that little, wise breast, and I threw my arms around his neck, and hugged him close to me, to let him know that I was reconciled, and that our friendship was born afresh in perfect understanding.

It was now quite dark, well into the night, and the woman had taken our orders for dinner, when Eumolpus, the poet, knocked at the door.

'How many of you are there?' I called out, peeping through a chink in the door to see if he had brought Ascyltus with him. When I saw that Eumolpus was alone, I opened the door and let him inside. He threw himself straight on to the bed, and when he looked up and saw Giton waiting at the table, he nodded and said:

'I like the look of your Ganymede. Today should be a good one for us.'

I was hardly pleased at this curious statement, and began to be afraid that I had let someone just like Ascyltus into the house. Still, Eumolpus persisted, and when Giton passed him a drink, he said: 'I prefer you, my boy, to all the men in the bathhouse.' He downed his drink in one go, and began to tell the story of his evening at the baths:

'I was almost flogged tonight while I was washing myself,' he cried, 'all because I had tried to go round and recite poetry to the men, and they kicked me out as though the place were a theatre! After that, I wandered around every nook and cranny, and called out your name, "Encolpius!", in a loud voice. But then, in another part of the bathhouse, a naked young man was wandering too – he had lost all of his clothes, and he kept shouting for Giton, just as loudly as I was calling Encolpius.

'The boys were mocking me, copying my cries, but with the naked man, who kept calling "Giton! Where are you? Come back to me!", they all gathered round, a crowd of them, and applauded him, looking at him in admiration. See, the thing was, he had the most enormous cock – it was as though the man was attached to the penis, not the other way around! Well, that was a well-equipped young man. No wonder he found help in no time at all – some Roman knight, notorious for his thirst, gave the young man his clothes, and took him home to enjoy him, I suppose. And here I was, naked, and the attendant wouldn't return my belongings to me. As the saying goes, a polished wick is much more useful than a polished wit …'

As Eumolpus was telling his story, my expression kept changing: I laughed at my enemy's bad luck, and then was left annoyed by his successes. Still, all the while, I kept quiet, saying nothing, just passing the food around for dinner, and pretending that I had no skin in the story at all.

NERO
& SPORUS

SUETONIUS, *THE TWELVE CAESARS*, 'THE LIFE OF NERO'

This is a thoroughly nasty passage. It contains abuse, assault, misogyny, incest and bodily degradation. Here, Nero is described through a litany of obscene or grotesque acts. He burns through all morality, loosing himself into a frenzy of unfettered sexual desire, maiming and abusing as he goes. There is no mention of love, or romance. This is desire in its most feral form, and is not condoned at all. It gives us a brutal insight into the terrifying combination of power and lust, and shows how it tears through its victims like a wildfire, incinerating not just personal but also cultural morality in its path.

Incorrigible, ruthless, Nero was not satisfied with abusing boys or seducing married women. He raped Rubia, the Vestal Virgin. Once, he nearly managed to make Acte his wife by bribing some high-ranking friends of his to lie under oath, swearing she was a royal by birth. Another time, he castrated a young boy, Sporus, trying to make a woman of him, and then carried him off, dressing him in a bridal veil, and married him. After the ceremony, and with the whole court in attendance, he took Sporus home and treated him as he would treat a wife on her wedding night. Some have made a joke, saying that the world would have been a better place if Nero's father, Domitius, had married that sort of wife.

Nero dressed Sporus in the finest clothes, like an empress, and took him to all the markets and fairs of Greece, and then through the Street of the Images in Rome, where he bent occasionally to give Sporus a tender kiss.

Everyone knew that Nero had a passionate longing for his own mother, Agrippina, but he was kept from consummating it by her enemies, who were afraid that Agrippina's power would be too great if the pair came together. Nero even found a concubine to add to his group, who everyone said was the image of his mother. Some say that the mother and son did have sex. They said you could see it from the state of his clothes – all dishevelled and with telling stains on them – whenever they left their carriage.

Nero was so amoral that, after he had defiled every part of his own body along with the bodies of others, he invented a sort of game. He was put into a cage, and dressed in the skins of wild animals, and then he would be released. Like a beast, he would pelt forward towards men and women who had been tied to stakes and, in a frenzy of lust, he would attack their genitals. After he had worked himself up into an ecstatic pitch of desire, his man, Doryphoros, would finish him off.

After this, Doryphoros married Nero, just as Nero himself had once married Sporus, and on their wedding night Nero went so far as to imitate the cries and screams of a woman being deflowered. I have heard from some men that Nero was convinced that no part of any man's body was ever chaste or pure; in fact, everyone, for Nero, was hiding some sort of secret vice. Because of this, if anyone ever confessed to obscene acts and desires, Nero would forgive them all their other crimes.

THE
INVINCIBLE
GENERAL

PLUTARCH, *MORALIA*

This extract from the 'Dialogue on Love' in Plutarch's *Moralia* discusses various passages from mythology and history, all in praise of Eros. Although ostensibly part of a dialogue, there are few interruptions, and the speaker ranges through his subject with a loose, associative logic. We hear of a warrior, Cleomachus, and his bravery, and how his beloved witnessed him die in battle; and we also hear of many other lovers and their beloveds, not least Heracles.

As in Plutarch's *Lives*, where the author relates the story of the 'Sacred Band' of lovers – an undefeatable army – here Love is taken to strengthen Lovers, and to live 'side by side with courage'. In fact, it might even be argued that in this extract Plutarch goes even further. Rather than Eros being a supplement to Ares, the god of War, Eros usurps Ares, encouraging people to great acts of bravery. Though, in Ancient Greece, women did not participate in the military, Plutarch argues that Eros can inspire them to warlike acts, and even to warlike deaths. This is a compassionate and humane passage, full of wonder for the power of affection and human bonds. Love is also presented, at the end, as a great improver, making those possessed by it more generous, more kind and more forgiving.

And now, consider how superior Eros is in the sphere of war. He is not idle, as Euripides said; he has done service in the field, and does not spend his nights 'sleeping on the soft cheeks of girls'. A man filled with love has no need for Ares, the god of war, to fight his enemies. If he has Eros with him, he is ready, at the call of his friend, 'to cross through fire and rough seas and through the winds themselves'. When, in Sophocles' play, the sons of Niobê are being shot at and are dying, it is not a helper or an ally that one of them calls out for, but his lover. And I'm sure you all know the story of Cleomachus of Pharsalia, and how he came to fall in battle?

'We don't know that story,' said Pemptides and those gathered around him. 'But please, we would be glad to hear it.'

'It is worth hearing,' said my father, and continued to tell the tale.

At the time when the Lelantine War against the Eretrians was at its zenith, Cleomachus came to help the Chalcidians. The Chalcidian infantry seemed strong enough to hold, but they had a hard time keeping the enemy's cavalry at bay. So his allies asked that Cleomachus, who was renowned

as a noble man and a man of courage, be the first to charge. Cleomachus asked his beloved, for the handsome boy was by his side, if he would witness the battle. His beloved said that he would, and embraced him and kissed him tenderly and placed his helmet on his head for him. Cleomachus was filled with pride then, and walked to the head of the army of Thessalians he had brought to aid the Chalcidians, and he charged into the enemy cavalry with such strength and bravery that they were thrown into disorder, and when the rest of their soldiers also fled, the Chalcidians took a thrilling victory.

But among the spoils there was a bitter wound. Cleomachus was killed in the charge. Even now, the people of Chalcis will point to a huge pillar in the marketplace of the town, under which sits his tomb. Whereas, in the time before the battle, the people of Chalcis had derided the love between men and boys, after Cleomachus had won victory and died for them, they honoured this sort of love above all others.

There is some disagreement on this story. Aristotle tells us that it was a different man, one of the Chalcidians, who was embraced by his beloved before the battle, and provides as evidence this popular song from Chalcis:

O noble boys, O handsome lads,
don't hide your love, don't be shy
before brave men – for in Chalcis,
Love is looser of limbs, and thrives
side by side with courage.

In your city, Thebes, is it not customary for a lover to give his beloved a full suit of armour when the boy becomes a man? And wasn't it Pammenes, a man well versed in Love, who changed the order of the infantry, saying that Homer knew nothing about Love when he organized the Achaeans by tribe and clan rather than by lovers and beloveds? He knew that Love is the only invincible general; for men in battle will desert their tribesmen and relatives and even, god knows, their children and their parents; but no enemy can drive themselves between a lover and his beloved.

It was this bond that led Thero of Thessaly to raise his left hand to a wall, draw his sword, and cut off his own thumb, challenging his enemy to do the same. And another man, who had fallen on his face in the midst of a battle and was just about to be dealt a fatal blow at his enemy's hand, begged his rival to wait a moment so that he could turn around, so that his love should not see him wounded from behind.

And it isn't only the most warlike nations, the Cretans and the Boeotians and the Spartans, who are the most amorous, or the most susceptible to love, but the great old heroes too: Meleager, Achilles, Aristomenes, Cimon and Epaminondas. In fact, Epaminondas loved two young men. Their names were Asopichus and Caphisodorus. Caphisodorus died with Epaminondas at Mantinea and is buried by his side, and Asopichus was such a fierce warrior that the man who eventually killed him won honours from the Phocians.

As for Heracles, it would take too long for me to list all his loves. Even to this day, lovers worship and honour Iolaüs, exchanging vows over his tomb, believing him to have been beloved by Heracles. Some also say that Heracles saved the life of Alcestis to please Admetus, her husband, who had been one of Heracles' beloveds. They also say that Apollo loved Admetus, and served him every day for a year.

It's lucky, in fact, that I've remembered Alcestis. Women don't have much to do with Ares, the god of war, but when they are possessed by Love, they are led to acts of courage

beyond the bounds of their nature. Sometimes, it's fatal. If we give credence to mythology, we can learn from the tales of Alcestis, Protesilaüs and Eurydice that one of the few gods whose commands are obeyed by Hades is Eros. As for all the others, as Sophocles says, 'He shows no bias or kindness / to anything but justice.' To lovers, though, he shows respect. It is for lovers alone that Hades ceases to be implacable. So, my friend, although it is a good thing to be initiated into the Eleusinian mysteries, I say that the celebrants of Love's mysteries have a better place in Hades.

It isn't that tales from myths are the sole guides of my thinking, or that I believe everything in them, only that I cannot discredit them entirely. On one point, at least, the myths teach us well. When they say that lovers are able to return from Hades to the light of day, they are speaking the truth. There are, in the clouded rivers even of Egyptian mythology, bright particles of truth, though a man must be sharp-eyed and discerning if he is to light on them and to draw the right conclusions from their evidence.

Anyway, we are moving from the point. I would like to speak about Love's kindness and his goodwill and how he favours humankind. I do not mean the favours he bestows on those who are loved (these favours, I think, are perfectly clear to everyone); but rather, the favours he bestows on lovers themselves. Euripides, though he was well experienced in love, only scratched the surface when he wrote that

Love makes a poet of a man.

Love makes a person sharp and intelligent, even if he was slow before. Love makes a coward brave, just as men make soft wood strong by hardening it in a fire. Every lover is transformed into someone generous and high-minded, even if beforehand he was narrow-minded and selfish. Like iron in the fire, the worst qualities of the lover are torched away, so that, once Love has possessed them, the lover is purified. He is happiest when he is giving to his beloved, and doesn't care about receiving gifts himself.

You will remember, I think, the tale of Anytus, the son of Anthemion, who was in love with Alcibiades. One night, he was throwing a big dinner for his friends, and Alcibiades stormed into the room, drunk with wine, and took half the goblets from the table and walked off with them. Anytus' friends were shocked and irritated, and said, 'That boy is so rude! Look how he treats you!' Anytus smiled and shook his head. 'Not at all. In fact, he is very kind to me; for where he might have taken everything, he has left me half.'

A MOONLIT MISSION

VIRGIL, *THE AENEID*

This is the tragic, bloody story of Nisus and Euryalus. Unflinching in its focus on the gory, pitiable violence of warfare, Virgil's *Aeneid* is a litany of deaths, described in repeating, almost incantatory imagery. Here, Nisus and Euryalus, an inseparable pair of skilful warriors, make their way under cover of night into an enemy camp. There, they kill a group of drunk, sleeping soldiers, and Euryalus loots a shiny helmet. However, on their way home, they are spotted: Euryalus' helmet shines in the moonlight, and the pair are driven into a thicket of woods by a band of cavalry. What is notable here is how Virgil's language shifts from the language of war to the imagery of romantic love. Euryalus, the young beloved, is killed; and Nisus, heartbroken and full of rage, lays his own body over his love. The contrast between the show of brutal masculinity and the tender ending is a heartbreaking vision of the tragic disruption and brutality of war, and of the enduring love between men.

All across the Earth, the creatures of the world
were blanketed in sleep, their troubles hushed by night;
but the Trojans were up late, deliberating in the small hours
about the fate of the land, their routes to salvation, and who
among them should be sent as a messenger to Aeneas.
Between the fields and the camp, their spears glinted
in the moonlight; if they moved, their shields flashed. Nisus
and Euryalus, together, arrived suddenly, out of breath:
'Let us in! We come with news that must be heard.'
Iulus stood up quickly, and told them to speak, and Nisus said:
'You must give us a fair hearing, sons of Aeneas. We are young,

but the words we say are urgent. The Rutulians have fallen
into a deep slumber, dazed with heavy wine, and we have spied
a place to ambush them. There is an opening where two roads
meet by a gateway close to the sea. In that place, the ring
of watch-fires is broken, and the black smoke rises to the stars.
Give us the chance, and we'll return laden with spoils, the blood
of our enemies spilled behind us. We can trust that road.
We have hunted often in those secret valleys, and have seen
the first houses of the city, and know the river well.'

                        It was old Aletes
who replied, exclaiming the powers of the gods of Troy,
and thanking them for putting such courage into the breasts
of the young Trojans. He took Nisus and Euryalus
by the shoulders, and clasped them tightly, the tears
brimming in his eyes. 'What prize could I give you?
What honour in the world could reward you both?
The gods will grace you for your bravery, but soon
Aeneas and Ascanius will follow with blessings
and with endless gratitude.' Here, Ascanius spoke up:
'Even more,' he said. 'My whole life hangs uncertainly
on my father's return. By the gods and their holy shrines,
every piece of my fortune I lay into your hands, and my truest word
into your lap: call my father home, let me see him
and all sorrows will end. Here, take these two silver cups,
and these two chairs, and these weights of gold, and take
this antique bowl, given as a gift from Dido of Sidon.
If the day comes when we capture Italy and take the crown,
I'll take from the spoils this horse, this shield and the crimson
plumes, and give them all to you, Nisus, along with a dozen
women and a dozen prisoners of war, and all the land
King Latinus owns. As for you, Euryalus, you're just a boy,

but a boy to be honoured nevertheless. I take you
into my heart and into my arms, and will share every glory
with you, no matter what the season.'

To this, Euryalus answered:
'So long as the hand of fortune favours us, I will be equal
to such words. But there is one thing more urgent
to my mind than all those gifts: I am in grief for my mother,
one of Priam's line, who all Troy and all Acestes' city walls
could not keep from being by my side. But now, sweet mother,
I must leave her, and she knows nothing of the treacherous
time I am entering, and I have not found words to tell her,
or even to bid her farewell. I tried, but I could not bring myself
to see her weep. And so I ask just this of you: comfort her,
bring help to her helplessness, consolation to her desolation.
This would be the most precious gift you could give to me.
Let me carry that hope in my heart, and I shall set off from here
more boldly, more bravely, into the dangers that await.'
Euryalus spoke so tenderly that the gathered Trojans wept.
There was such love for his mother, and Iulus, taking his hand,
assured him that he would do everything he could.
'She will be to me as my own mother, Euryalus.
Any woman who could have raised such a son
deserves all our gratitude. And I promise you,
by this head on which my father swore all his oaths,
that no matter what happens, my gifts will pass down
to your mother and to all your kin.' Iulus wept as he spoke,
moved by love for his own father, and took from his shoulder
a gilded sword, fashioned by Lycaon of Knossos
into an ivory sheath, and Mnestheus gave to Nisus
a lion's hide, and Aletes took off his own helmet
and placed it on Nisus' head.

Well-armed now, the two men
began to march, escorted by the Trojans to the gates,
the sound of earnest prayers burdening the warm air.
Foremost among them was Iulus, walking now
with a man's spirit, and bearing troubles
beyond his years. He gave the two men countless
messages to deliver to his father, but the wind
snatched them, and scattered them all
to the cold, indigo sky. Nisus and Euryalus
moved stealthily, crossing the ditches in search
of the enemy camp, hidden under the night's
dark curtain. The holm oaks swayed their quiet shadows
and the steps of the men were hushed by the soft green fronds
of the ferns. Then, where the trees opened to the bright
high notes of water, they found them: all those men
in their drunken sleep sprawled across the grass,
the up-tilted chariots unattended along the riverbank,
their reins and the wheels splayed, and then
more soldiers, tangled together among a litter
of armour and of drinking vessels. 'Now, Euryalus,'
whispered Nisus, 'now is the hour to show our mettle.
This is our road. Keep watch behind us for attackers.
And as a man in the wilderness might clear a path
through the overgrowth, I'll go forward with my sword
and slaughter these men and make a way for you.'
Not a moment after he spoke, he plunged forward
and drove his sword into the chest of Rhamnes,
who was fast asleep, swaddled in thick blankets.
A man, who was once a prophet, loved by a king,
now choked on his own blood. Quickly, in a flash
of metal, Nisus stabbed three sleeping servants
and then Remus' armour-bearer, and then his charioteer,

who was lying at the foot of his steed. All those soft
slumbering necks he sliced open with his sword.
Once he had started, he didn't stop: a jet of crimson
shot from the neck of their lord as he tore it off,
and the beds and the bare soil were soon drenched
in thick, shining blood. Then Lamyrus, then Lamum,
then young Serranus, who had played all night
with his friends and had been happy and drunk.
Like a famished lion, driven wild by hunger, tearing
through a fold of sheep, Nisus mauled and maimed
all that soft flesh and dripped with its blood. Behind him,
Euryalus matched his fury. Like a fire blazed bright
by a sudden wind, he tore his way through the sleeping men –
Fadus, Herbesus, Abaris and Rhoetus. The latter woke,
his eyes fixed in terror on the scene. Quickly, he hid in panic
behind a wine-vat, but his shaking breath gave him away:
as he rose, Euryalus sunk his whole blade
through the man's chest and drew it out smeared
with blood. Rhoetus choked: a river of blood
and wine and vomit poured through his mouth.
Euryalus pressed on, quiet and unmoved through the crowd
towards the followers of Messapus. The watch-fires
were dull, only glowing embers now. They flickered
in the night beside the tethered horses. 'Let's go,'
Nisus said, seeing the lust for blood, the greed
for violence in Euryalus' eyes. 'Dawn, to us, is no friend,
and soon her pink, betraying light will creep up
on the horizon. We have had our vengeance.
We have cut a clear path.' So, the pair moved,
and left a clatter of silver armour behind them.
But Euryalus took as a prize Rhamnes' medallions
and his gold-studded belt. Caedicus had given these

to Remulus, to remind him how their friendship endured
through absence. When Remulus died, he passed them
to his grandson, and then they had passed to the Rutulians
as spoils of war, and now Euryalus snatched them up
and placed them on his own shoulders. Then, he took
Messapus' helmet with its lavish plumes, and wore it
as they left the camp, and headed for safety.

Meanwhile, as the rest of the army waited, a dispatch
of cavalry – three hundred men, their shields glinting
in the night, led by Volcens – was sent out from their city
carrying a message for Turnus. They neared the camp,
and as they passed they saw Nisus and Euryalus turning
down a path. It was the stolen helmet, shining
in the moonlight, that betrayed Euryalus. 'You men,'
shouted Volcens. 'Stop! Where are you going, armed
at night? Who are you?' The men, startled, bolted
into the woods, trusting themselves to the gloom
of the branches. The riders split up, surrounding
the wood and blocking all its paths. The forest was dense,
tenebrous with undergrowth and thicketed with ilex.
Every line of sight was obscured by brambles
and the lush, whispering curtain of the holm oaks.
Only the tracks of the deer showed the faint, glimmering signs
of a path through the glade. Euryalus, cloaked
in the shadow of branches, panicked with fear.
He lost his bearings; he lost the path. Nisus, though,
was sure-footed and plunged ahead, not looking back.
Without knowing it, Nisus escaped. He came out, panting,
to a place of high-fenced cattle pens where the moon
was cold and bright, and when he stopped, he turned
to look for his friend. 'Euryalus! Where did I leave you?

Which way shall I go now?' Even as he spoke,
he started to retrace his steps, his eyes scanning
the quiet thickets, looking for the route. Then
he heard the sound of horses, then the quickening barrage
of hooves in pursuit, and then a loud shout loosed
from the trees. It was Euryalus. Wrong-footed
in the fibrous dark of the wood, confused by the sudden
barrage of the hooves, he had been caught and carried off.
He was struggling against the soldiers, crying out.
Nisus, what can you do? How can you rescue your friend?
If you attack, what weapons will you use?
Should you throw yourself among the barrage
and the thicket of swords and rush through blades
and take those furious wounds and die for him?

Nisus drew back his arm and tilted his spear to the heavens.
Seeing the moon's silent witness, he prayed: 'You, O you, Goddess,
glory of the stars, watcher of the groves, be here for me
and Euryalus, help us in our hour of need. If ever my father
brought offerings to your altar, or if ever I hung my spoils there
in your temple after a hunt, or fixed them to your sacred eaves,
let my spear splice the air, let it throw those men into havoc.'
When his prayer was finished, he launched the spear with the force
of his whole body – it tore through the curtain of the night
towards Sulmo, and sunk into his back, sending a sharp splinter
through his diaphragm. Sulmo keeled over and spewed a stream
of hot blood from his chest. His thick legs convulsed with pain.
As the enemy lost control, darting in all directions, looking
for the attacker, Nisus – bold from this first success – prepared
another spear, and took aim. The band were still in panic
when the second blade sliced, whistling, through the air
and drove into the forehead of Tagus, rupturing his brain.

The silver spear stuck there. Its metal warmed with blood.
Volcens was savage with anger, but nowhere among the trees
or the night could he see the attacker – his anger surged
left to right, boiling, but found no direction, no outlet,
until his eyes lighted on Euryalus. 'You!' he cried, 'you
and your blood will pay for both these deaths.' And he drew
his sword with a shimmering sound from its sheath
and rushed forward. Nisus panicked, his mind white
with terror, and he broke cover, shouting, 'I'm here, it's me,
I'm the attacker, aim here! He is innocent, I swear
with the sky and the stars as witness, his only offence
is to have loved too much the wrong man.' Nisus
was still calling out these words when the sword was driven
with awful force through the ribs of Euryalus, slicing
his white breast apart. He rolled on the earth. The blood
bloomed from his sweet body. As when a flower is cut
by the plough, his neck drooped, and his head fell limp
against his shoulder. Nisus' grief tore through him
like a fire. He ran blindly into the thicket of soldiers
seeking Volcens, and his mind thought only of violence
and revenge. Like a bolt of lightning, his sword
flashed against the soldiers who tried to hold him back.
He cut his way with rage until he found Volcens
and, face to face, drove his sword deep into the man's
open mouth. So, when he felt his own life seeping away,
he cut off the life-giving breath of his enemy. Still,
Nisus' torso was pierced all over, his strength was failing,
and his last act was to throw himself on to the body
of his love, and he rested there, on the lifeless
Euryalus, until death drew his own life from him.

ORESTES
& PYLADES

EURIPIDES, *IPHIGENIA AT TAURIS*

Euripides, one of the great tragedians of Ancient Greece, wrote *Iphigenia at Tauris* between 414 and 412 BC. There is a story before the beginning of the play: Iphigenia, a young princess, was about to be sacrificed by her own father, Agamemnon, but at the last moment the goddess Artemis swapped the princess for a deer, saving Iphigenia and taking her away to the land of the Taurians. Here, the princess was made into a priestess at the temple of Artemis, and given the awful role of ritually sacrificing foreigners. Iphigenia, horrified by her fate, longs to go home, or to send a message to her family to tell them she is still alive.

Here, Orestes (the younger brother of Iphigenia, who has killed his mother Clytemnestra to avenge his father) and his dearest friend, Pylades, arrive at the temple of Artemis. They are unaware of the identity of Iphigenia, and have been sent by Apollo to steal a statue of the goddess from the temple, but know that, if they are seen, the priestess will sacrifice them. When the two are captured, Iphigenia learns that they are from Argos, and says that she will spare one of them if they will take a letter back to Argos for her. Orestes asks that he be sacrificed, feeling responsible for their journey, and wanting to save Pylades from this gruesome fate. In this scene, Orestes' and Pylades' words are spoken, and the words of the Chorus are sung.

CHORUS [*to Orestes*]: We sing a lament for you, stranger. These drops of sanctified water, sprinkled on your hair, will soon blend with your blood, and minister to you.

ORESTES: Please, don't sing those songs for me. This isn't something to be pitied. Goodbye, goodbye, strangers.

CHORUS [*to Pylades*]: As for you, young man, fate shines on you. We sing a happy song for you. We rejoice. Soon, you will tread on your native soil.

PYLADES: Fate shines on me? You rejoice? How can I rejoice, how can fate be happy, when my friend is sent to die?

CHORUS [*to Pylades*]: O! What a cruel journey awaits you.

CHORUS [*to Orestes*]: O! You are destroyed! What a cruel death awaits you.

CHORUS: Ah! Which of your fates is worst? My mind is torn in two. Shall I mourn for you, or for you? Poor heart, which man deserves more of your cries?

ORESTES: By the gods, Pylades. Are you struck with the same thought as I am?

PYLADES: I don't know, Orestes. What are you thinking?

ORESTES: Who is that young woman? She knows so much about Greece. She questioned me about the troubles at Troy, and the returns of the Achaeans, and about Calchas, who reads the birds as omens, and about Achilles, too. Did you see how her face turned to pity when she heard about Agamemnon and his wife and their children? She must be from Greece. I think she is of the Argive race, which means she's a foreigner here, too. Otherwise, why would she be sending a missive there? The way she asked her questions – the anxiety in her face – it was as though her own fate was joined to the fate of Argos.

PYLADES: I had been thinking the same thing, Orestes. But doesn't everyone know the stories of the kings?

Especially those who travel. Still, there's something else eating away at my mind …

ORESTES: What is it? We can work it out together.

PYLADES: It's the shame, Orestes. The shame of being alive when you are dead. It would be unbearable. For so long, we have sailed together. We ought to die together, the two of us. It will seem cowardly when I go back to Argos and to the valleys of Phocis, if I go there without you. People will think that I betrayed you, that I abandoned you and sailed off home alone. God, they might even say that I killed you – that I plotted your death and took advantage of your family's troubles, since I was the one who married Electra, your sister, and it would be me who would inherit your fortune.

I must breathe my last breath beside you, Orestes. I should die with you, and be burnt on the same pyre, because I am your friend, and you are mine.

ORESTES: Hush, Pylades! I can bear my own fate. I can endure it. But I cannot bear my grief to be doubled, to have your life placed on top of mine. The things that you are afraid of – shame and dishonour – would be mine, if I were the cause of your death. You are my dearest friend. You have helped me through my life's troubles.

It is no hardship for me to give up my life, since it is the gods who have willed it. But you are blessed. Your family is not, like mine, polluted and cursed. It is pure and prosperous. If you are saved, and live beyond me, and my sister bears your sons, my name will live on. You can save my name, and my father's house, and give to us a future.

Please, Pylades: save yourself, and go and live in my father's house. Here, take my hand and promise me that, when you arrive back in Greece, and in Argos, you will make a small tomb for me, and a small memorial with my name on, so that my sister can make offerings there, and shed her tears over the stone. Tell everyone at home that I died at the hand of an Argive woman. Tell them it was at an altar, and that she sprinkled sanctified water on my brow.

And please, Pylades, when you return home, and see how Electra has been deserted, and how lonely my father's house is, do not abandon her.

Now, Pylades, I must say goodbye to you, my most loved friend. Take my hand. As children, we played together, and as young men we hunted side by side. You have shouldered my griefs, and helped me through my life. I was Apollo's toy – that god is a prophet, but he lies, and he drove me away from Greece, and I trusted him, and killed my own mother and so, wretch that I am, I must die. Farewell, my friend. Farewell, Pylades.

PYLADES: You will have your tomb, Orestes, and I will never betray your sister. If it is possible, I will love you even more after death, and hold your memory close in my life. Still, couldn't a change come yet? Is there not time still for you to be saved?

ORESTES: Hush, Pylades. Apollo's words are no use to me now. Here, look: the woman is coming towards us from the temple.

PAUSANIAS
ON LOVE

PLATO, *THE SYMPOSIUM*

This passage from Plato's *Symposium* is one of the most famous pieces of writing from the classical world. In it, Pausanias offers his celebrated speech on Love, focusing on the love between men and younger boys, and distinguishing between 'Heavenly Love' and 'Common Love'.

The Greek valorization of pederasty – usually depicted as a nurturing relationship between an older man and a free-born boy – is prevalent in many of the tales in this book. Though this was by no means the only sort of relationship between men in Ancient Greece, its educational role was central to the culture. Younger boys – aged about fourteen to eighteen – were courted, and took the passive role in sex. Such cultural practices make us uncomfortable now. So, too, does the implicit misogyny of Pausanias' speech, which once again praises male homosexuality as an ideal partly because it excludes women.

It is wise to remember that these words are put into the mouth of Pausanias by Plato. Indeed, Pausanias was a real person, and likely to have been much more inclined towards exclusive homosexuality than others in the Greek world. In other words, there may be a level of characterisation at play here. Nevertheless, the impact of this speech has been long-lasting and significant in queer history. Oscar Wilde, to take just one example, referenced it in his own famous speech during his trial for gross indecency. The 'love that dare not speak its name' is 'such as Plato made the very basis of his philosophy … It is that deep, spiritual affection that is as pure as it is perfect.'

We all know that there is no Love, no Aphrodite, without someone to love. If there was just one Aphrodite, there would be a single Love; but since there are two of her, so it follows that there must be two Loves. Does anyone doubt that Aphrodite is double? There is the older one, who is the daughter of Uranus, and who has no mother. She was born of Heaven, and so we call her Heavenly. And then there is the younger one, who is the daughter of Zeus and Dione: she is called the Common. In this way, it follows that each type of Love is named after the goddess who partners it, who is its fellow-worker, and so there is Heavenly Love and Common Love. Of course, all gods must be praised, but it is important to distinguish the different characteristics of these two.

There is no action that, in and of itself, is either noble or ignoble. Look around you: whether we drink, or sing, or debate, none of these activities could be called noble in itself, but only becomes noble in the doing of the thing, and in the way it is done. When we do these things nobly, so they become noble; when they are not done properly, they are base, and wrong. It is the same with the act of loving. Love is not always noble or deserving of praise. It is only deserving of such when we are compelled to Love in a noble way.

Common Love is rightly named: it is haphazard, undiscriminating, and is felt by undiscriminating people, like those who love women as well as boys, and whose love is attracted to bodies rather than to souls. These people often choose lovers who have little intelligence; in fact, they seek them out. Their only desire is in accomplishment and quick satisfaction. They do not care if they love rightly or wrongly; they love like chaos and without distinction. The origin of this is the younger god. She is where their love derives and finds its partner, and she is part female and part male.

Heavenly Love, on the other hand, finds its fellow-worker in the Heavenly goddess, who has no touch of the female, only the male; and who is also the elder of the two, and so is less fickle, less abusive and more mature. Those who are inspired by this Love are enamoured by males, who are more robust, and have a greater share of intelligence. Even within those who are attracted to boys, it is possible to recognize those people who are motivated only by Heavenly Love, for these people seek out boys only when their minds are fully formed, in the later stages of puberty. This is because those people who seek out such boys are ready to be always beside them, and to share their lives together. They do not take advantage, or try to trick the boy, who may still be young and apt to be foolish, nor to make a mockery of his trust before making off with another.

A law should have been enacted to put an end to affairs with young boys. Their outcomes, after all, are uncertain, and may end in a waste of time. Who among us can tell how a young boy will end his development? Will his body be virtuous or vicious? And what about his soul? Good men, though, are self-governing, and follow this rule of their own accord. Those lit by the Common Love, however, ought to

be made to follow the rule, just as we try our best to stop them sleeping around with free-born women. After all, these people bring reproach and scandal to the door of Love, and taint its possibilities, so that there are even those who say it is wrong to satisfy a lover at all. The people who say such things are misguided by this reckless loving, but as I have said, there is no action that is wrong in and of itself, so long as it is done rightly.

The conventions of loving in other cities are easy to explain. They have been laid out clearly and straight-forwardly. But in Elis, and in Boeotia, where the people have no skills in speech, everyone simply agrees with the idea that it is right to satisfy lovers. They do this in order to save themselves the need to articulate their positions, or to use the art of rhetoric. In Ionia, though, and in many other places, they live under a different rule, and it is agreed that love-affairs are a thing of shame. This is because they have no democracy, and they live under despotism. All philosophy, all sports, and training of the intellect, they are told, are a thing of shame. No doubt, the rulers are afraid of what would happen if the people began to think, or to have ideas, or to forge the social bonds that these activities, especially the act of loving, are apt to foster. It is a lesson that all oppressors learn. Didn't Aristogeiton's love, and the strength of Harmodius' affection, bring the power of the Athenian tyrants to an end? So, in any place where there is a rule that the satisfaction of lovers is wrong, this can always be traced back to the defects of the rulers, to the combination of the government's lust for power, and the cowardice of their subjects. Likewise, in places where all acts of loving are seen as equally right, this can be traced back to the laziness of the rulers and their sluggish minds.

But here, in our city, our conventions are better, though they are more complex. Consider, for example, our common saying that it is better to love openly than in secret, especially if your beloved is noble and virtuous, and even if they are not beautiful. And think, too, of the way love is received by the populace. The encouragement we give to lovers is a sign to them that there is nothing shameful in their loving. It is thought by everyone that it is a fine thing to find success in the pursuit of a boy. Only to fail in the pursuit of love is thought a disgrace. So, when a lover is trying to catch his boy, our culture celebrates him, and gives him the freedom to do extraordinary things for love which, if done under any other name, would be met with reproach.

Imagine, for example, if someone was trying to get money out of someone else, or trying to gain political office or another position of power, and was prepared to act as lovers do in pursuit of their beloveds. Imagine that this man dropped to his knees in supplication, imagine if he begged and made promises and spent all night sleeping on someone's doorstep like a dog, and was prepared, in effect, to undergo submission. His friends, surely, would talk some sense into him; they would censure him; and no doubt his enemies would do likewise, mocking him for his lack of self-respect. But if the man is a lover, and does all these things for his beloved, he is celebrated and praised for his behaviour. The strangest thing of all is that only a lover is forgiven by the gods when he breaks a promise. A lover's oath, they say, is no oath at all. So, it is true that both gods and mortals have given absolute freedom to the lover.

From all that I have said so far, you might assume that, here in our city, loving and showing love are actions held in the highest esteem. Still, it happens that when boys become

beloveds, their fathers put them under the watch of tutors, to prevent them talking to those who desire them. It even happens that the boys' friends and playmates call them names if they see that they have become beloveds, and adults don't intervene in the bullying. If you look at this side of the story, you might assume, by contrast, that loving and showing love are held in disgrace.

Here, I think, is the truth of the matter: loving is no simple thing and, as I have said before, it is neither right nor wrong in itself, but only in the way it is done. To love wrongly is to gratify a wicked man in a wicked manner. On the other hand, to love rightly is to gratify a good man in a noble manner. By 'wicked', I mean the lover inspired by the Common Love, who longs for the body, but not the soul. You see, this lover is never constant, because he loves something that is always changing: as soon as the beauty of the body fades, the lover 'flutters away, and is gone', leaving all his speeches and his promises behind. Whereas the one who loves the soul remains constant throughout his life, since he unites himself with something that remains constant too.

Now, this gives some explanation to our customs, which are a wonderful way of encouraging the right sort of love. This is why, without contradiction, we encourage our lovers to chase their beloveds, and we encourage those beloveds to run away. It is a sort of sport, which reveals which sort of lover the lover is, and which sort of lover the beloved is. This is why we attach a sort of shame to those beloveds who allow themselves to be caught too quickly. There is no chase, no competition, no trial – only when time intervenes between the pair can we determine which sort of love is being made. This is also why we consider it shameful to be enamoured and caught up by a lover's money, or a lover's status. If the boy is caught by these things, he may have been cowering at the thought of being crushed, or he might love gold and political success more than love itself. Neither gold nor power are permanent, and so any bond based on their foundations is unstable, and liable to collapse.

There is one way left in which, according to our customs, a beloved may satisfy his lover. As I have said, a lover's willingness to submit himself to love, and to his beloved, to undergo all sorts of enslavements to him, is not counted as scandalous or debasing. This is because the purpose of this submission is to increase the virtue and wisdom of the beloved. So, I say, if a lover is willing to put himself at another's service, to place his integrity into another's hands, but he does this in the hopes that he will make the beloved better in wisdom, or some other virtuous thing, then there is no debasement at all, and no humiliation.

It is time, now, to compare these two rules; the one dealing with the love of boys, and the other dealing with the love of wisdom and other virtues. In doing this, we shall see whether it is a good thing or not for a beloved to satisfy his lover. For, when a lover and his beloved come together, each of them guided by their own rule – the lover being justified in committing himself to the service of the beloved, and the beloved being justified in showing affection to the lover who will make him wise and virtuous – and if these rules can both be followed through, with the lover imparting virtue, and the beloved desiring it, then it is truly right and noble for the love-affair to happen.

To have one's hopes deceived is no disgrace; but if these two rules are not followed, and if the intentions of the lover or the beloved are wrong, then the love that is made is wrong. Imagine, for instance, that a boy thinks that his lover is rich, and admits his advances in the hopes of becoming rich himself. In that case, if the lover turns out to be poor, and the boy does not get any money from the match, what he does is still wrong. This kind of boy reveals his own character: he would go beyond the bounds of propriety in order to be rich. In the same way, imagine that a boy thinks his lover is a good and virtuous man, and admits his advances in the hopes of learning from him, and becoming good and virtuous himself. If the lover turns out to be a wicked man, there is no disgrace to the beloved in being deceived. On the contrary, this beloved has revealed something good in his own character: he would do anything, for anybody, in order to gain in virtue and wisdom, and there is no better motive than this. It is right, and virtuous in itself, to join with a lover in the hope of becoming virtuous oneself. This, after all, is a love inspired by the Heavenly Love, with the heavenly goddess as its fellow-worker; and this love is a universal good, of value to the city and to the people, because it compels lovers to pay attention to their own virtue, and it compels beloveds to do the same. All other forms of love are inspired by the other love, the Common Love.

These, Phaedrus, are the thoughts I am able to offer you, called as I am on the spur of the moment, towards a discussion of love.

GAYS FOR DEMOCRACY

ARISTOTLE, *THE ATHENIAN CONSTITUTION*

This is the story of two lovers, Harmodius and Aristogeiton, who became known as the tyrant-slayers, or 'Tyrannicides'. Famed for plotting against and murdering the tyrant Hipparchus, the two men became the preeminent symbols of Athenian democracy. There are conflicting accounts of how the plot was pulled off, and Aristotle recounts some of them here. Thucydides claims that daggers were hidden in ceremonial myrtle wreaths, but Aristotle says that this idea is anachronistic.

Here, Aristotle tells of two brothers, Hippias and Hipparchus, and of Hipparchus' murder at the hands of the lovers. After the attack, Harmodius is killed, and Aristogeiton is arrested and subjected to a long torture, during which he accuses various high-powered and noble people of conspiring in the plot.

Because of their station, and their age, Hippias and Hipparchus had assumed control of affairs. Still, Hippias was the older of the two, and the most statesmanlike, and so he headed the government, and Hipparchus, who had a youthful air and was amorous, fond of literature, brought poets to Athens.

Now, there was someone called Thessalus, who was much younger than the pair: he was headstrong, and prone to insolence. He was the one who wrecked the house. For, after some time, he fell in love with a man named Harmodius. When Thessalus' approaches were rebuffed, his anger flared. He was embarrassed, and lost all restraint. One day, in a wounded outburst, he saw Harmodius' sister, who was going to be a basket-bearer in a festival procession.

To get in her way, Thessalus shouted at her. 'Your brother,' he said, 'is a pansy, a limp-wristed flirt.' The shame of the insult ruined the woman's honour, and she was excluded from the procession.

It's no surprise that Harmodius, hearing of that attack, turned against Thessalus. The insult, not only to himself but to his sister, burned inside him. So, not long afterwards, he entered into a plot with a lover named Aristogeiton.

When the time came for the festival of the Panathenaea on the Acropolis, the men involved in the plot were keeping watch on Hippias, one of the two men in charge of the government. Hippias was waiting to be received by the procession, and Hipparchus, his brother, was directing it.

The men watched for a while, waiting for the right moment. Then, across the street, they spied one of their own accomplices talking to Hippias. They panicked. Was their plot being betrayed? Before they could be arrested, the watchers rushed down without waiting for the others, and took hold of Hipparchus and murdered him. In an instant, all their careful plans were thrown into havoc. Harmodius was killed on the spot by the guards, and Aristogeiton was arrested, and was to die later, after suffering a lengthy torture.

While he was being tortured, Aristogeiton shouted accusations against the most distinguished families of Athens, and against many people who were friends with the tyrants. At first, the government could find no trace of the plot. There is a current story that Hippias made all the people taking part in the procession give up their weapons, so that he could find those who were concealing secret daggers, but this cannot be true. After all, at that time, the processors did not carry any weapons.

Some historians say that Aristogeiton accused the friends of the tyrants so that the tyrants themselves might murder innocent men, committing a sin against the gods. Others say that Aristogeiton was telling the truth under torture, and was betraying his accomplices.

In the end, when all his efforts to be released by death had failed, Aristogeiton promised to give information about more people, and asked for Hippias' hand, to symbolize a promise. But as soon as Hippias took the man's hand, he fell into a frenzy of anger, having taken the hand of his brother's murderer, and so, quick with hatred, he took out his dagger and killed him.

IT'S TOUGH
BEING A GIGOLO

JUVENAL, *SATIRE IX*

Juvenal's *Satires*, which number sixteen in total, are ironic, sometimes angry comments on morality and society. Full of biting
commentary, filtering through vices and virtues, the poems were
written over the turn of the first and second centuries AD. In
Satire IX, we witness a conversation between the poet and a male
prostitute, Naevolus, who complains about his patron and the
lack of appreciation he gets for his work. Naevolus is looking
haggard, past his prime, and Juvenal recalls the days when the
man used to sleep with countless women and their husbands,
keeping marriages alive through the pleasures of adultery.

JUVENAL: I cannot read your face, Naevolus. A cloud
has moved across it, shadowing your skin. Marsyas, the satyr,
looked better after his flaying. God, you look like the slave Ravola,
caught in the act, his beard sopping, going down on Rhodope.
I can't believe how miserable you seem. Even a salesman
no one trusts, who can't shift his shares, has half a smile.
Where did these wrinkles come from? These tired eyes?
I remember when you were the toast of any table, telling jokes,
taking life as it came. You're a different man now. The state of you!
Your hair's like a hedgerow; your face like an old sheep
caught in a bush. Years back, your skin glowed like a sunrise –
now it's bristled with wiry curls. You're wasting away, Naevolus.
How much weight have you lost? Look at you shivering!
It's like your soul's eating you up from the inside. Strange,
isn't it, how a life can part in the middle, splitting its course …

It wasn't long ago you were cruising the Temple of Isis
and the shrine of Ganymede, picking up the easy women.
God, you bedded them by the dozen – and you bedded
their husbands too, if I'm not mistaken!

NAEVOLUS: It's true. That life has paid many a man's rent,
but I've never had my share of profit from it. Sometimes,
I'd get a greasy cloak to save my toga, or some shoddy, garish
shirt, or a ring without a hallmark, but not much else. See,
all men are ruled by the Fates, and the Fates guide our privates
as much as they do the rest of our bodies. If your stars
are set against you, it doesn't matter how big your cock is.
It doesn't matter if Virro drools at the sight of your tool
or if long love-letters arrive every week, protesting
that 'every man loves a stud'. There's nothing worse
than a tight-fisted pervert. 'I paid you this for that,
I gave you two coins today, I'll give you more tomorrow.'
God, I'm sick of it. Add it all up and it barely comes
to five thousand. Compare that to my list of services.
You think it's easy, or fun, cramming my dick
into someone's guts until it's stopped by last night's dinner?
A slave who ploughs his master's field has an easier job
than the one who ploughs his master. 'Tell me,'
I say to him, 'you used to fancy yourself a pretty lad,
a latter-day Ganymede, fit to carry the cups of the gods –
will you ever cough up, ever pay for your own desires?
Doesn't a beautiful boy deserve a parasol, or scented amber
on his birthday, or presents to open while he lolls
on his daybed some showery spring morning? Tell me,
sparrow, who are all those pastures for? Those bright
estates, those endless fields you keep? Even the kites
get tired, flying the length of them. And those vineyards

on the ridge of Cumae, the rows of purpling grapes budding
through the empty lands of Gauras … No man's vats
are fuller with rich vintages, and yet, not an acre
nor a drop for me.' 'You're a brazen man to say that,'
he replies, but my rent calls on me to ask, and my slave
as well. I only have one, and soon I'll need another slave,
and how will I feed them both? What will I do when the winds
come in the winter and strip the trees? How will I answer
the shivering of their feet and the knocking of their knees?
Will I say, 'Be patient, boys? Summer's cicadas
are just around the corner?' Virro, you can discard
all the other favours I've done you, all those itches
I've scratched, but if I hadn't been so dedicated,
so good at my job, your wife would still be a virgin.
God, the girl was halfway out the door, tearing up
her marriage vows, when I got her into bed! I spent
the whole night inside her just to change her mind –
and the sound of you wailing in the garden didn't help.
Didn't you hear the mattress creak, the wood groan,
your lady gasping out? Never mind. Adultery's saved
many a marriage. You couldn't count the services
I've done for you. Didn't I give you a son and daughter too?
That's right. You'll raise them as your own, as little adverts
for your own virility, but you know the truth. Still,
you're a father now, and that's another gift from me.
Maybe there'll even be a third kid on the way soon.

JUVENAL: That seems like a fair complaint, Naevolus.
And what was his reply?

NAEVOLUS: He ignores me completely. It's not long
until he's traipsing after some other two-legged donkey

like myself, sniffing the air. But please: don't say a word.
The last thing I need is to make an enemy of a man
who exfoliates himself with a pumice stone. He's mad.
He told me all his secrets, and now he's acting
like I've spilled them all. Juvenal, he wouldn't think twice
about having me knifed, or of torching my house
at night. So keep quiet. For a man that rich,
no poison costs too much.

JUVENAL: My poor, poor Corydon. Don't be naive.
What secrets can a rich man keep? If his slaves
aren't already gossiping, then his horses will, or his dogs,
or his doorposts or his statues … God, if he barred
all his windows, drew the blinds, locked the doors,
put out his lamps and turned every guest from the house,
still the tavern-keeper two streets down would know
by dawn what he'd been up to the night before. Slandering
the rich is everyone's favourite pastime. The lashing tongue
is the best revenge for the master's whip. Anyway,
there's always some drunkard at the crossroads pouring
tales into a passing ear. Gossip and secrets everywhere.
It's not me you should be keeping quiet, but them.
Pay the rumour mill no mind. The tongue is the grindstone
of a bad slave, churning out rubbish all day long –
but the worst of all is a man who can't escape the talk
of his own servants. It's their way of placing the yoke
back around his neck.

NAEVOLUS: That sounds wise, my friend. But tell me,
where do I go from here? I feel caught in a bluster
of past years and all their wasted hopes. Life, like the seasons,
hurries our little flower to its close; and while we drink

and play with garlands the sharp wind is coming in
and sending our youth to seed.

JUVENAL: Don't worry, Naevolus. So long as these seven hills
stand fast around us, the rich men will keep flocking here;
the ships bring new cargoes every day. In the meantime,
have you tried chewing colewort? It keeps the flesh in heat.

NAEVOLUS: Ah, keep that for someone else, Juvenal.
The Fates that rule my life are only too pleased that my cock
can keep my stomach from rumbling. O, my poor
household gods – don't I burn incense for you? Don't I adorn you
with garlands and with offerings of corn? Will I ever save
enough to keep me from the beggar's crutch when I am old?
Ah, for a little pot of gold, or a set of silver platters and a clutch
of strong Bulgarian men to carry me on their shoulders
through the crowds. Maybe a painter to take my portrait,
maybe a nice engraver. Gods, it's a sad little prayer. Whenever
I speak to Fortune, she seems to stopper her ears with wax.

IN PRAISE OF IMPERFECTIONS

CICERO, *ON THE NATURE OF THE GODS*

This passage of speech, preserved by Cicero, records a statesman who was enamoured with an actor named Roscius, who had a squint in his eye. Here, he takes a slight detour away from the subject of the divine and moves instead on to the world of human love. It is preoccupied with subjectivity and beauty, and how things that are otherwise deemed to be imperfect – such as a blemish, or another bodily feature – become ornaments to our desire. How would we construct a perfect human, when it is our imperfections that make us so beautiful? The anecdote recorded here suggests that some cultural ideals are revealed as false when love's light passes over them.

You mustn't think I'm lacking in self-esteem, but if I were to
express myself freely, I would have to say that I am not more
beautiful than the bull that Europa rode; yet the question
here is not about our intellect, or our powers of oratory,
but the beauty of our outward forms. If we were all free to
invent our own forms, combining the parts of others, would
you object to looking like Triton, the merman, who we often
see riding on sea creatures attached to human bodies?
But this seems like slippery ground on which to build an
argument. After all, the force of nature and instinct means
that no one who is born human wishes to be anything but
human. I dare say an ant wouldn't wish to be anything
but an ant, either.
  Still, what kind of man would we wish to be?
It is rare enough to be beautiful. When I was in Athens,

for example, there was hardly one beautiful man to be found
in each division of the training corps. Ah, I can see you
smiling, but it is true. Either way, those of us who enjoy the
company of young men, as the ancient philosophers allow
us to, often find even their imperfections to be charming.
'Alcaeus admires even a mole on his beloved's wrist.' A mole
is a defect of form, but Alcaeus thought it was beautiful.
Quintus Catulus, the father of our own colleague and friend,
had a soft spot for your fellow townsman, Roscius. In fact,
he wrote the following verses in his honour:

> Once, walking out at dawn, I stood
> to pray before my god, the rising sun –
> and what did I see but Roscius, standing
> to my left, lit by the glowing orb. Forgive me,
> powers of heaven, if I say the mortal
> seemed more beautiful than the god.

HOW TO SNAG
A LOVER

TIBULLUS, *ELEGIES*

At the beginning of this poem from Tibullus' *Elegies*, the speaker asks the phallic god Priapus about his skills in seducing beautiful young men. He is besotted with a man, Marathus, whose reticence torments him. Racked with an intense sexual desire, he is seeking advice, and the god replies, telling him how to court young men, how to please them, and how best to love. The passage is beautifully layered, favouring lists and turns, lamenting the passage of time, the onset of age. It lifts off, at the end, in praise of poetry, and shows a generous and empathetic openness to the lovers and to the sufferings of love.

'Tell me, Priapus – so that a canopy of leaves
might protect you, and the sun's spears or the snow's
blades never fall harshly on your head – what ways
do you have to charm the boys? It's hardly as though
your beard is glossy, or your hair well groomed.
I've seen you walking naked all winter, and naked too
when the season of the Dog-star parches the ground.'
This is what I said, and the rustic child of Bacchus,
carrying his curving bill-hook, answered me:
'Don't rush to trust those pretty boys. They always
offer a home for love to grow. One might please you
in the way his hand grips a horse's rein. Another lad
in the way his pale chest parts the water as he swims.
And then, one might catch your eye with his bravery;
another with his modesty, the blush of his boyish cheek.
But don't give up, even if they resist. Over time,

their necks will yield to the yoke. Even lions
have been tamed into man's company, and water,
through the years, makes a rough rock smooth.
The sun, over the season, swells and sweetens
the grapes, and the year drives the constellations
turning in the heavens. And don't be afraid
to make promises: the perjuries of love are void.
The winds carry them away, scatter them on the face
of the sea. Jove made it so, nullified their power,
so love's folly might swear anything in a fit of passion.
Diana is complicit as well. She'll let you swear by her arrows
without coming to harm; and Minerva, too, by her hair.
But you have to be quick. Do it slow, and all will be lost.
A youth's youth flashes by, and time does not repeat
or return. Isn't it the same with the earth, who loses
her purple colours quickly; and the poplar, stripped
of her leaves by the cold. Even a prized horse, who once
shot from the starting gate, is abandoned when age
has wasted him. I've met many a young man, harrowed
by the coming years, regretting how he spent his youth.
The gods are cruel. The snake can shed his skin
and be young again, but the Fates give no such grace
to man. Only Bacchus and Phoebus have the prize
of constant youth. No doubt you'll give yourself
away to your beloved: love, after all, wins most
through compliance. Even if he wants to walk
for miles through the burning summer, you'll go.
Even if the rainbow brims, and the sky is brushed
with mauve, and a storm is gathering. If his wish
is to cross the high salt-wave, you'll grab an oar
and steer the boat for him. And there'll be no word
but "yes" from you, even if your untrained hands

are calloused from the work. If, around the deep glen,
your beloved wants to stage an ambush, your shoulders
will bear the hunting nets. And if, to pass the time
in pleasure, he wishes to practise his sword, play lightly;
leave your side unguarded often, so he may take
the victory. After that, he'll be gentle with you.
Snatch a kiss. He might resist, but he'll let you take it,
and it won't be long until he brings it to you unbidden,
without shame, and begins to hang his small arms
around your neck. Still, our wretched time has bred
boys to look for gifts. Whoever first taught the ways
to sell and purchase love should have his bones pressed
beneath a heavy stone. Love, instead, the muses
and the poets. The measure of verse has the trick
of keeping Nisus' hair in lilac hue. Without poetry,
there would have been no ivory of Pelops' shoulders.
The one the muses tell of will live for ever, so long
as the earth brings forth the oak trees, and the rivers
flow, and the heavens cherish their burden of stars.
And whoever has no ear for the music of the muses,
who sells love for a price – let them follow the chariot
of Idaean Ops, and wander three hundred cities
until their limbs are cut. Kind Venus gives us room
for love's wreckage.' This is what Priapus said. 'Her sights
shine brightest on those who beg, and weep, and feel.'

DIONYSUS &
PROSYMNUS

CLEMENT OF ALEXANDRIA, *EXHORTATION TO THE GREEKS*

This is a fragmentary tale, not told in full by any Greek author, though hinted at by several. Dionysus is searching for his mother, Semele, who is in Hades. He wants to rescue her, but does not know how to gain entrance to the underworld. What follows is a strange and strangely moving tale of promises and lust. The story is reputed to be at the origin of various, apparently indescribable, nocturnal ceremonies that took place by the Alcyonian Lake in ancient times. There is a rumour that Clement of Alexandria, the author of this account and an early Christian theologian, may have been trying to discredit the pagans when he wrote this story. Perhaps he was suggesting that they were unable to control their lusts. It is, admittedly, quite bizarre; but it doesn't appear crude to me. Rather, it seems to speak of a sort of sexual afterlife, and of the powerful imaginary world of someone who wishes to conjure the sensation of a lover back from beyond the grave.

Dionysus, god of the revels, was desperate to make his descent into Hades, but he did not know the way. By the Alcyonian Lake, he found a man, a shepherd by the name of Prosymnus, who offered to help him. He would row Dionysus into the middle of the lake, showing him the entrance to Hades, but he wanted something from Dionysus in return.

Some might have thought the thing was a shameful one, but Dionysus didn't. He had no qualms with granting it. 'When I return from Hades,' he said, 'I give you my word, I will let you make love to me.'

So, after Prosymnus guided him to the entrance of the underworld, Dionysus went in search of his mother, Semele. But when he returned, his mission achieved, he could not find Prosymnus anywhere by the lake shore, and was told that the shepherd had died. Dionysus was beside himself: with grief, and with lust. He ran over to Prosymnus' tomb, and knelt down before it. How would he fulfil his oath to the handsome shepherd who had helped him?

Then, he saw a fig tree growing from the tomb, and cut down a branch of it. Carefully, with a blade, he shaped the branch into a perfect phallus, and closed his eyes, thinking of Prosymnus, whose body might have grown through the tree. He picked up the dark-wood phallus and, lying on the shepherd's tomb, entered himself, fulfilling his promise, and thinking all the time of Prosymnus.

AFFAIRS OF THE HEART

PSEUDO-LUCIAN, *AMORES*

The *Amores*, also known as *Affairs of the Heart*, is a work of dialogue. Because scholars are not sure if it should be attributed to the Syrian satirist Lucian or not, it is usually given under the name 'Pseudo-Lucian'. The *Amores* is devised in the genre of contest literature. Two speakers, Lycinus and Theomnestus, are then joined in a second dialogue by Callicratidas and Charicles, who come forward to pick up on the debate, and to continue to compare the love of women and the love of boys. Ultimately, they conclude that the latter is the most honourable, or the most desirable.

Just before this extract, the romantic gaze on the life of boyhood is framed in misogyny, with Lycinus contrasting 'the evils associated with women' with the pure, noble and virtuous ways of an idealized young man. Whereas women, in Lycinus' speech, are suspicious, fickle, and described with dripping disdain, the life of young men, and the love of young men, is painted as true, divine and wise. We have come across these prejudices before, with the same sense that homosocial love and friendship between men is best because it is purest, free from the taint of women. It should serve as an apt and still urgent warning to us that even this extract's poetic vision of queer love is one based on exclusion.

Indeed, the passage seems to invite us into conversation with the past. Taking the example of Orestes and Pylades, it searches for its own historical precedent, giving an insight into the ways that, even in ancient times, homoerotic love sought justification and cultural validity in the ancient tales of the heroes.

He rises, when the sun rises, from his bed, washes away the night and the sleep from his eyes with pure, cold water, and after fastening his shirt and his clothes, he leaves his father's hearthside with his head bowed, not looking up to meet the eyes of anyone who happens to pass him in the streets. In his wake, a company of attendants and tutors follow him, each holding the instruments of virtue with which he will be trained into manhood. Not the vain instrument of the comb, nor the mirror that, with no artist present, can reproduce the visions it sees, but the tablets for writing, and the books that hold the tales of ancient deeds, and the well-tuned lyre, should the day call upon him to visit the music master.

And, after he has worked hard at his lessons in philosophy, and trained his intellect for the day, moving step by step through the toils of education, he turns then to the exercise of the body. For this is a youth who loves Thessalian horses; and soon, after he has broken himself in, as one might do a colt, he is given range to practise, peacefully, the arts of war, perfecting the javelin throw and the angled flight of the spear. Next, there are glistening hours in the wrestling school. His taut body, still growing into its form, gleams under the high noon sun. The dust lights on him, and he sweats through it, his body wrapped against another boy's tanned skin.

He washes himself clean again afterwards, plunging himself into the bath waters, and eats a meal before returning to his studying. The schoolmaster might ask him about history: which hero did this, which wise man said such and such a thing; who was it who cherished justice and temperance in the olden days? These virtues wash through his soul, brightening it, nourishing it as it grows; and at the close of day he rests, and falls into a well-earned sleep.

Who could not fall in love with a youth like this? Who could be so blind, whose faculties so numbed as to resist him? How could any of us fail to love a boy who is like Hermes in the wrestling school, like Apollo at the lyre, like Castor on horseback? In short, one who works each day towards the virtues of the gods, but with a mortal body? For my part, I pray to the gods that, throughout my life, it might be my pleasure to sit beside him, to hear him talk to me in that sweet voice, to go out into the world with him and be always part of his life.

No one would blame me for wishing that a lover like that might travel through life, from youth to old age, without sorrow, never caught in the fickle snares of Fortune. But, if his body should experience what bodies do – if sickness should touch him at any time, I would be by his side, and if ever he sets out through stormy waters, I would sail with him. And if some tyrant bound him in chains, I would chain myself beside him. All his enemies will be my enemies, and all his friends would be dear to me. If there were thieves or mobs on the roads, and if they rushed at him, I would steel myself as his protector; and if, god forbid, he should die, I could not bear to live without him. I would tell all those I love to make for us a common resting place, so that my bones would lie with his, and the dust of our bodies would be joined for all time.

And I am not the first to say these things: all the wise heroes made them their laws, and often their dying words testify to the love of friendship. Phocis, for example, brought Orestes to Pylades when they were only infants. Taking the god of love as their intercessor, the two boys sailed through life in the same ship. Both of them did away with Clytemnestra, as though they were sons of Agamemnon, and Aegisthus was killed by both their hands. Pylades suffered when the Avengers coursed Orestes, and stood alongside his friend in the trial at court. And their love was taken with them beyond Hellas, they journeyed with it to Scythia, and when one of them was injured, the other was his nurse. And when they arrived at the land of the Tauri, the Fury of matricides was there to welcome the foreigners, so when the natives clustered around the two men, Orestes was struck to the ground with madness, and as he lay there, Pylades

'Soothed away the foam from his lips, and stroked
his tender frame, and wrapped him in a princely robe.'

He acted not just as a lover, but as a father to him. When it was decided that one of the pair must be killed, and the other must be sent

to Mycenae to deliver a letter, each of them begged to remain, to spare the other, knowing that each of their lives depended on the survival of the other. Still, Orestes refused to bear the letter, saying that Pylades was the one who should do it, and in this way he showed that he was the lover, rather than the beloved.

'For it would break my heart if he were killed.
I must be the one to suffer the Fate's hand.'

And, not long afterwards, he says:

'Give him the letter. I'll send my love
to Argos; and he will live long after me –
for that, I would let any man take my life.'

This is often the case. It happens that, when the love born into us in childhood develops and matures, being inflected with reason, the one we love returns our love, so in perfect times we become pure mirrors of each other, and the source of the love, the light and the image, becomes impossible to tell apart. Why, then, do you say that this is something modern, some indulgence of our own day, when it has been passed down to us from the gods, and from the oldest histories? We are glad to have received something as precious as this; we approach its shrine with openness and with the most reverent hearts. Any man is blessed, as the wise word goes,

'Who has beautiful boys and shining steeds;
and the old man eases into his years the best
when he is beloved of the youth.'

It is no surprise that Socrates' teachings were honoured from the seat at Delphi on which the Pythian priestess sat, or that the oracles

of the god told us that 'Of all men, Socrates is the wisest.' For, along
with all his other virtuous discoveries, which have brought wisdom
to life over the years, did he not also say that the love of boys was
the greatest blessing?

So, one should love youths just as Alcibiades was loved by Socrates,
the older man sleeping with the younger, fatherlike, under the same
cloak. And I would decorate the end of my speech with the words
of Callimachus, which should be heard by all:

> 'May you who light your longing eyes on boys
> love the youths as Erchius told you to, so that,
> in its men, your city may be blessed.'

Minding this lesson, young men, make sure to be caring in your
approach to noble lads. Do not, for the sake of quick satisfaction,
throw away the love that might develop there. And do not, until
you yourselves have matured, put on the show of affection, but turn
your worship instead to divine love, and keep constant throughout
your life. For those among us who love in this way have no stain
on our conscience, and enjoy a sweeter life and a sweet and shining
reputation after death. For, if the philosophers are to be believed,
heaven has room for men like this, and by walking through death's
door with a pure heart, and a pure record in love, this human life
may be made immortal.

I WON'T STOP
KISSING YOU

THEOGNIS, *ELEGIES*

The lyric poems of Theognis – a Greek poet who wrote during the sixth century BC – have been split into two 'books'. The second book, which consists of one hundred and sixty-four verses, are predominantly homosexual in their subject matter. These are poems addressed to beautiful boys, or expressing the pains and joys of being in love. The scholar K. J. Dover tells us that the separation of Theognis' work into two 'books' probably happened in the Middle Ages, when these intense expressions of homo-sexual feeling were moved apart from Theognis' other poems, which dealt with the ethics of honesty and truthfulness.

In this poem, the poet addresses a beautiful beloved. He asks the boy to take pity on him, to alleviate the pain of his desire. It is a pining and startlingly vulnerable poem of unrequited love, and makes us feel that particular bodily pain of being consumed by longing for another.

Since Cypris has blessed you, my boy,
with grace, and has brought all the men
around you, drawn to your flame,
listen to me awhile. Love is a heavy burden,

and only you can lift it. Beautiful Cyprian,
my love is like pain to me – and only you
can nurse it, can shine it, can make me
happy again. Take me, if only

for an hour, then set me back to work,
to wisdom, renewed. So long as I see

your face, I won't stop kissing you. Even if
to kiss you meant to die, I'd never stop.

It's a beautiful thing for you to heal me –
and, since I love you, it's only right
that I should ask. Someday, it will be you
who kneels before a handsome boy

with violets in his hair, and longs
for love. And you'll be happy, then,
if he gives it to you. Beautiful lad,
all lovers are happy who love happily

and then journey home, and sleep
the whole day long beside a handsome boy.

PHAEDRUS
& SOCRATES

PLATO, *PHAEDRUS*

In this lyrical, rhythmic passage from Plato's *Phaedrus*, Socrates delivers a speech on the madness of love. As with *The Symposium*, this text is written as a dialogue, this time between Phaedrus and Socrates. Before the extract, Socrates speaks of reincarnation: souls grow wings, he says, and eventually return to where they came from. When we are in love, Socrates says, we are possessed by a vision of beauty on earth that is heavenly, and our lost wings begin to grow back. Here, Plato (via Socrates) uses the example of love between men. With the image of chariots and horses, the passage describes the tension between restraint and desire, and the contest between the lover and the beloved when they are possessed by love. It is written in long, carefully measured sentences, capturing this sense of energy and control, so that, in a way, it mirrors the beautiful and tortuous tensions of love itself.

Now, since the beloved is blessed with all kinds of services from his lover, as though he were a god himself, and since the lover is true, and is really in love, and since the beloved feels warmth and affection for his lover, who serves him – though perhaps at one time he spurned his lover, shamed by his schoolmates for yielding to the older man – nevertheless, as time passes, his youthful mind and the hand of destiny deliver him into the arms of love. For, after all, fate's law says that evil can never be a friend to evil, and that good must always be a friend to good. So, when finally he yields to his lover, and has granted him sweet company and conversation, the lover is astonished. Who is this boy,

who is so good, and godlike, and youthful? The lover begins
to think that all his other friends, and even his relatives,
are no company at all in comparison to his beloved.

And, as their intimacy gathers, and perhaps one day
the lover comes close to the beloved in the gymnasium,
or in the general gatherings of life, the bright springs
of that fountain named 'desire' by Zeus, when he fell in
love with Ganymede, flow over the lover. And some flows
into him, and some, when he is filled, flows out of him,
overflowing; and just as an echo or a breath of wind
rebounds from smooth surfaces, returning to its source,
so the stream of beauty passes back into its issuer, through
his eyes, which are the inlet of the soul. When it arrives
there, it reanimates the hollows of his lost feathers, setting
him aflutter, making his wings grow, and soon the soul
of the loved one is, in turn, filled with love.

He is in love, then, but he doesn't know who with.
He is at a loss. He does not know, and cannot say, what
has happened to him. Like a man with a contagion,
he is unaware that, when he looks at his lover, he is seeing
himself, as though in a mirror. Only when his lover is with
him does his anguish cease; and in his lover's absence he is
filled with longing, and is longed for, and he feels his love
flowing back to him, like an image of his lover's love,
requited. He has the wrong name for it, though: he believes
it is friendship, but it is love.

The strength of his desire is similar to his lover's,
but not quite so strong. He longs to see his lover, to touch
him, to kiss him, to lie down with him, and it is not long
before these things are brought about. Now, as the two lie
together, the lover's unruly horse has something to say to his
charioteer. In return for his many troubles, he wishes for

a little pleasure. And the unruly horse of the beloved is quiet, and says nothing, but swells up with passion and draws the lover into an embrace, and kisses him, caressing his body as his best friend; and when they are lying down together, the beloved would not refuse his lover anything. But, presiding over this, there is a pull of modesty and reason, resisting.

So, if the better elements of the mind (which lead us into a well-ordered, philosophical life) prevail, so the lovers live a life of harmony and happiness on earth, masters of themselves, resisting those elements that let evil into the soul, and opening the soul up to the elements of goodness. And, if this happens, when the lovers die they become winged and light, having won one of the true Olympic contests. Not human wisdom, nor the inspiration of the gods, can bring to a person any greater blessing than this.

But, if they choose to live a life less noble, devoted not to the love of wisdom but to the love of honour, then perhaps when they are drunk, or careless, those two unruly horses inside the lovers will catch them off-guard and seize them, and bring them together in a bliss many people hold in high esteem. And, once this is done, they carry on doing it, again and again, though sometimes infrequently, because they know the blessing of their whole mind does not shine down on it. These two spend their lives as friends, but their connection is not as great as the other pair. They believe, during the course of their love and when it has passed, that they have given and received the most binding pledges, and that these pledges will never break, and that they will never grow to hate each other. When these lovers die, they have no wings, though their wings have begun to grow, so even these are rewarded for the madness of love, and shall never pass into darkness or travel beneath the earth.

These two will live a happy life in the light, journeying together, and – because of their love – when they receive their wings, both of them shall be given matching feathers.

These blessings, so great, so divine, will come to you through the friendship of a lover, my boy. Whereas the affection of someone not in love is alloyed with good sense, and comes with many rules of conduct, and benefits in mortal life, this sort of affection ties us to the world, to life, and narrows us, making us wanderers on the earth, and leaving us, in the end, under the earth for nine thousand years.

EPILOGUE

LUKE EDWARD HALL

Since setting up my creative studio in 2015 I have worked on a variety of projects – more of these than I can count on two hands have been 'classical' in flavour, and without a doubt more than a shade queer. There was the design for a safety curtain for English National Opera: blown up to nearly eighteen metres tall, my curtain featured a pink-lipped Orpheus, the legendary poet and musician, playing his violin in a moonlit, violet-tinged glade beside a lyre-playing Apollo, god of music and dance, golden arrows flying overhead. I have painted vases, platters, plates and tiles with mythological beasts and deities, columns and pediments and architectural fragments. I have daubed spear-throwing athletes dancing across the bottom of a swimming pool in Portugal and splashed Bacchic scenes on hallway walls in Belgravia. With Rubelli, the famous Venetian manufacturer of fabrics, I have produced a range of textiles with links to the ancient world. Here a woven cloth glittering with repeating rows of heads of Antinous, Emperor Hadrian's favourite; there a linen printed with watercolour sketches of blowsy red roses, busts and naked statues. I've done shirts and slippers, a red wine bottle, exhibitions in Athens, and I even named my graduate menswear collection of shirts and blazers, wide-leg trousers and woven wicker crowns Endymion, after the Aeolian shepherd king. I provide this list simply to point out the extent to which I've buried myself in classical myth and magic.

As a kid I loved a good story. I loved spells and monsters. I craved caves and crashing waves, towering mountains and dark skies. Actually, I lived in a commuter town: mythology was a kind of conduit, it took me to a place otherworldly. The Greek and Roman stories appealed in particular, with their heroes and hunters and princes; flying horses; death and revenge; magic and temples and oh! So. Much. Beauty.

It goes without saying that my fascination with the classical world had, and still has, everything to do with its queer characters. Growing up, I loved the idea of enchanted islands, impossible journeys and sea monsters, but the concept of gay heroes (in love!) blew my mind more than talking centaurs did. When I was young, much of the finer details no doubt went over my head, but gradually I came to understand, and as I began to work through how I felt about my own identity, I found comfort and respite in these stories.

It is interesting to consider how queer characters were viewed in the classical world. Zoe Schulz explains in her essay 'Finding Queer Belonging in Ancient Mythology' how 'Queer Gods and Goddesses were worshipped, with their differences seen not as a reason for hate, but as a symbol of power and beauty.' The myths may sometimes be written off as outlandish, preposterous tales, but, as Schulz notes, 'the study of mythology suggests they reflect the deep-rooted beliefs of a society.' The myths, at their very core, remind us that queer people, in all their wonderful, magical diversity, have always existed.

It was the sense of belonging the myths gave me combined with their fantastical imagery that resonated creatively as well as personally all those years ago. Discovering the world of classical mythology lit a fire in me, and that fire has continued burning since. In fact, it burnt brighter than ever whilst I worked on this book. For the journey I've been on with this project, working with Seán's beautifully alive translations, has reminded me how incredibly moving, strong and important these stories remain. Although they were told thousands of years ago, they continue to offer that same sense of deep belonging for many LGBTQ+ people today.

Boy with a maiden's glance,
I call for you, but you never hear –
you do not know that you are the charioteer
of my soul.

ANACREON, FRAGMENT 360

Euralyus, child of the Graces, darling
of the changing year, it must have been Eros
and tender-eyed Seduction who nursed you
here among the rose-flowers.

IBYCUS, FRAGMENT 288

Once again, tossing a shining ball to me,
Eros has beckoned me to play
with a slender girl in bright sandals –
but she, well-made in Lesbos, turns
her face from me, my greying hair,
and stares instead at another girl,
her lips apart in wonder.

ANACREON, FRAGMENT 358

FURTHER READING

Greek Homosexuality
Kenneth Dover (HARVARD UNIVERSITY PRESS, 1989)
A classic book, with no sense of squeamishness, Dover's *Greek Homosexuality* gives us detailed insights into the world of the Greeks through their poetry, art, fetishes, fantasies and legal codes. SH

Lovers' Legends: The Gay Greek Myths
Andrew Calimach (HAIDUK PRESS, 2002)
This slim volume collects together the key Greek myths and legends about love between men: Zeus and Ganymede, Heracles and Hylas, Achilles and Patroclus all make an appearance. LEH

Homosexuality in Greece and Rome: A Sourcebook of Basic Documents
Thomas K. Hubbard, ed. (UNIVERSITY OF CALIFORNIA PRESS, 2003)
A brilliant, compendious collection of writings, from lyric fragments to oratory, covering homosexuality in the classical world, with clear and incisive commentary. SH

The Seduction of the Mediterranean: Writing, Art and Homosexual Fantasy
Robert Aldrich (ROUTLEDGE, 1993)
Through an exploration of forty figures in European culture, this book suggests that the Mediterranean, classical and contemporary, was the central theme in homoerotic writing and art from the 1750s to the 1950s. LEH

Roman Homosexuality, 2nd Edition
Craig A. Williams (OXFORD UNIVERSITY PRESS, 2010)
Working against the 'industry of concealment' that obscured the study of Roman homosexuality in history, Williams's book is a brilliant study of power relations, masculinity, effeminacy and ancient identities. SH

Myths and Mysteries of Same-Sex Love
Christine Downing (CONTINUUM, 1989)
Downing aims to move away from the established notions of homosexuality to retrieve a more complex understanding of women's love of women and men's love of men. LEH

Sex On Show: Seeing the Erotic in Greece and Rome
Caroline Vout (BRITISH MUSEUM PRESS, 2013)
Illustrated with photographs of artefacts, Caroline Vout's book really
gets into the erotic gaze of the ancients, and is fascinating for how it navigates
the cultural codes inherent in the shapes and positions of the bodies
represented. SH

Picasso: Minotaurs and Matadors
John Richardson (RIZZOLI, 2017)
Published on the occasion of the *Picasso: Minotaurs and Matadors* exhibition
curated by John Richardson at Gagosian, London, this fully illustrated
catalogue examines the intersection of Picasso's bullfighting imagery with
his mythological and biographical compositions of the 1930s. LEH

Female Homosexuality in Ancient Greece and Rome
Sandra Boehringer, trans. Anna Preger (TAYLOR AND FRANCIS, 2021)
A book that caused a scandal when it was first published in France,
Boehringer's work gives an engrossing and sharp account of many of
the texts and characters you'll find in this book, from Ovid and Plato
to Martial's Philaenis and Anacreon's young lesbian. SH

Homer's Odyssey
Simon Armitage (FABER & FABER, 2007)
Originally commissioned for BBC Radio, Simon Armitage transforms
Homer's epic into a sequence of dramatic dialogues. His version is witty
and funny, and provided an excellent soundtrack whilst I worked on
drawings for this book. LEH

Sexual Life in Ancient Greece
Hans Licht, trans. J. H. Freese (ROUTLEDGE, 2000)
Fascinating and detailed, Licht's book explores so many aspects of the sex lives
of Ancient Greeks, from masturbation to fantasy, festivals to erotic games. SH

Jean Cocteau: Catalogue de l'exposition au Centre Pompidou
François Nemer (CENTRE GEORGES POMPIDOU, 2003)
A catalogue and companion to the Jean Cocteau exhibition at the Centre
Pompidou in Paris (September 2002 – January 2004), this is a well-thumbed
favourite from my studio library. I find Cocteau's mythological drawings
and murals endlessly inspiring. LEH

ACKNOWLEDGEMENTS

SEÁN HEWITT

I would like to thank Richard Atkinson and Sam Fulton for steering the ship with such precision and enthusiasm, and Amandeep Singh and Millie Andrew, who worked magic on the design and layout. Claire Péligry was an eagle-eyed and generous copy-editor for the final text.

Hannah Abigail Clarke did invaluable and thorough work on uncovering new source texts and helping me to navigate them, and with their expertise generously transcribed and glossed the originals from a wide range of books. Thanks, too, to Henry Eliot for offering important suggestions on extracts from the classical material. The beautiful design of this book is by Jim Stoddart, and it was produced by Taryn Jones and Joe Howse. I would also like to thank our campaign team, Matt Hutchinson and Liz Parsons.

I also owe a debt of gratitude to the librarians at Trinity College Dublin, for helping me navigate this material. For a long while, the words 'sodomy', 'sex', 'pederasty' and 'erotic' have occurred with frequency on my list of checked-out books, and no librarian has so much as batted an eyelid.

Thanks to Luke Edward Hall, for inspiring me with his vivid, gorgeous illustrations. A huge thank you, as always, to my agent Matthew Marland.

LUKE EDWARD HALL

I would like to thank our editor Richard Atkinson for writing to me (via our mutual friend Skye McAlpine – thank you Skye!) with the idea of creating a bold, colourful book focused on same-sex love in the ancient world.

Thank you to Sam Fulton for running the project in excellent order and for his early work on steering ideas. Our designer Jim Stoddart has done a fantastic job on the book's design, along with Amandeep Singh and Millie Andrew who worked on the layout. I'd also like to thank Matt Hutchinson and Liz Parsons from the Penguin publicity and marketing teams.

Thank you to Nadia Gerazouni and the team at the gallery I work with, The Breeder in Athens, who immediately responded to the book's magic with ideas for exhibiting the illustrations.

Special thanks to Seán Hewitt for his beautiful translations, which are often highly moving, sometimes funny, occasionally disturbing! The text is brimming with life, and each passage was a joy and a thrill to illustrate.

SEÁN HEWITT is a poet, memoirist and literary critic.
His work is inspired by the natural world, the presences
of the past, and the music of language. He lives in Dublin.

LUKE EDWARD HALL is an English artist, designer and
columnist. His colourful work is inspired by history, filtered
through a lens of irreverent romanticism. He lives in London
and Gloucestershire. His drawings and paintings are available
via The Breeder gallery, Athens.

PARTICULAR BOOKS
An imprint of Penguin Books

UK | USA | Canada | Ireland | Australia
India | New Zealand | South Africa

Particular Books is part of the Penguin Random House group of companies
whose addresses can be found at global.penguinrandomhouse.com.

First published in Great Britain
by Particular Books 2023
001

Set in Garamond MT Pro 12.5/16pt
Printed in Italy by L.E.G.O. S.p.a.

The authorized representative in the EEA is Penguin Random House Ireland,
Morrison Chambers, 32 Nassau Street, Dublin D02 YH68

A CIP catalogue record for this book is available from the British Library.

ISBN: 978–0–241–57573–4

www.greenpenguin.co.uk

Penguin Random House is committed to a
sustainable future for our business, our readers
and our planet. This book is made from Forest
Stewardship Council® certified paper.